THE
SCHOLASTIC CULTURE
OF THE MIDDLE AGES,
1000-1300

JOHN W. BALDWIN
The Johns Hopkins University

WAVELAND
PRESS, INC.
Prospect Heights, Illinois

For information about this book, write or call:
Waveland Press, Inc.
P.O. Box 400
Prospect Heights, Illinois 60070
847/634-0081

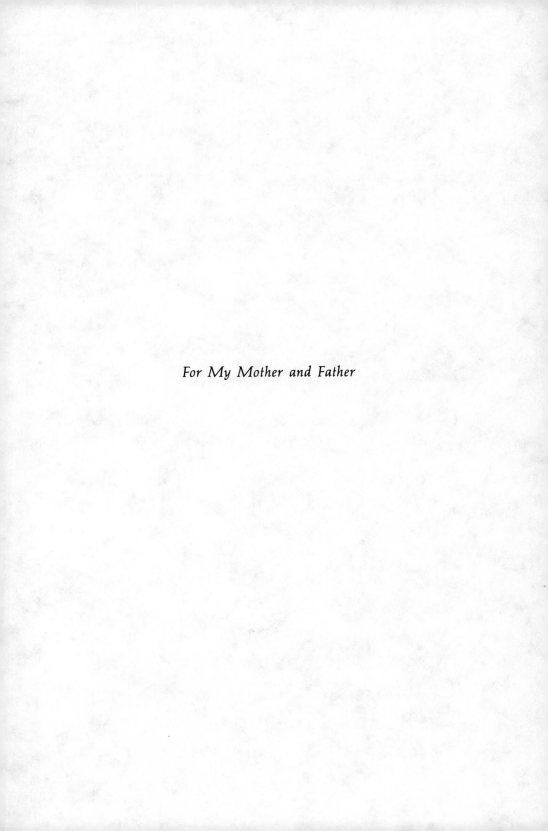

For My Mother and Father

PREFACE

To write a small book on a big subject requires explanation. Readers who are familiar with the list of suggested readings at the end of this volume will find little information that is new to them. It is my purpose and hope, however, that they will be introduced to a helpful perspective from which to view the subject. During the years I have taught at the University of Michigan and Johns Hopkins, I have become increasingly aware that the chief defect of cultural history as it is commonly practiced is the lack of a controlling focus. Cultural history has encompassed so much of human activity—art, literature, philosophy, morals, manners—that the historian has frequently felt himself compelled to record unrelated catalogues of data. To supply this missing unity, intellectual historians have viewed the culture of the Middle Ages as the product of the realist-nominalist debate, or as the acceptance of the ancient Classics in general or Aristotle in particular. Art historians have seen it as the contrast between the Romanesque and Gothic styles, and others have thought in broader terms of the accommodation of freedom with order. As a historian without training in these special cultural disciplines, I propose to make my contribution to the unity of medieval culture by emphasizing its common institutions. The operative word and controlling theme of this essay is "scholastic." Defined in a technical sense, scholastic is simply that manner of thinking, teaching, and writing devised in and characteristic of the medieval schools.

Unity of theme can best be achieved by ignoring what is irrelevant. To concentrate my efforts, I have limited attention chronologically to the eleventh through the thirteenth centuries and geographically to France and Italy, when and where, I believe, scholastic culture attained its apogee. I am aware that that complex civilization which we summarily call medieval contained other forms of culture not mentioned in this essay. The Carolingians, for example, in the early Middle Ages and the Burgundians in the fifteenth century produced distinct styles of civilizations. The culture of the Scandinavian north differed from that of the Mediterranean south. From the twelfth century the laity wrote vernacular literature distinct from the Latin writings of the clergy. The medieval intellectual heritage is also important for natural science and political theory as well as the arts, law, and theology. But I feared that if I pursued these subjects I would fall into the common temptation of cultural historians: I would write an essay too diffuse to convey a sense of the essential character of medieval civilization.

Despite the limitations of my theme, I have hoped that scholastic culture would nonetheless provide a large perspective for viewing the Middle Ages. To achieve this breadth I have forged a chain of related historical factors. By the thirteenth century cooperation between the Papacy and a strong French monarchy secured a measure of political stability conducive to peace, at least in France. Simultaneously, a sharp rise in population, an agricultural revolution, and a growth of trading activity brought increased prosperity to towns, and these in turn provided the economic and social context for schools and universities. As these educational institutions emerged, the teachers in them developed a common method of teaching and intellectual inquiry applicable to the liberal arts, medicine, law, and theology. This scholastic method not only was pertinent to the traditional academic disciplines but also was artistically expressed in Gothic monuments. In the Middle Ages, as today, each academic subject contained a considerable body of discrete and detailed knowledge. To treat these disciplines comprehensively is out of the question in an essay of this size. We would find the subject matter of each of the liberal arts and theology vast enough without pretending to approach the technicalities of medicine and law. I have therefore limited my attention to the common approach of these academic disciplines and have sought to illustrate this scholastic method by examining one doctrinal problem pertinent to theology and philosophy: the relationship between faith and reason. Although fundamental to medieval thinking, this issue does not sum up the problems of theology or philosophy, but it serves to exemplify the method which underlay medieval scholastic culture. Examples and materials could have been multiplied manyfold, but I trust that those included are sufficient to illustrate my thesis and yet brief enough to be read in one or two sittings. The first two chapters on the political, economic, and social setting are not intended to cover the subjects, but merely to prepare the reader who is largely unfamiliar with the history of the Middle Ages.

Among those who have helped with the writing of this book, I should like to recall the memory of a friend and colleague, now deceased, Adolf Katzenellenbogen, who read the chapter on Gothic art.

JOHN W. BALDWIN

CONTENTS

PLATES

MAPS

THE
SCHOLASTIC CULTURE
OF THE MIDDLE AGES,
1000–1300

On 12 August 1257, two Italian friars, the
Franciscan Bonaventure and the Dominican
Thomas Aquinas, were admitted as teaching
masters into the faculty of theology of the
university of Paris. Fourteen years earlier
Bonaventure had entered the Franciscan
convent, called the Cordeliers, to study under
the renowned English theologian, Alexander
of Hales. Two years later Thomas Aquinas
had come to Paris to hear the lectures of the
learned German Albert the Great at the
Dominican convent of Saint-Jacques. While
these two friar theologians were embarking
on a professorial career, a younger cleric from
Liège, Siger of Brabant, was finishing his
studies in the faculty of arts and was soon to
teach on the same faculty. In the same year
of 1257, Robert of Sorbon, the affluent
chaplain to King Louis IX, completed his
bequests to a college of poor students at
Paris, which later bestowed its name, the
Sorbonne, on the theological faculty and
eventually on the whole university. During
the same decade the master architect, John of
Chelles, was engrossed in plans for
completing the Gothic cathedral of
Notre-Dame. Since the west front, the two
towers, and now most recently, the
reconstruction of the nave had been finished,
John turned his attention to decorating the
facades of the north and south transepts.
Drawn to Paris from the north, east, and
south of Latin Christendom, Alexander,
Albert, Bonaventure, Thomas, and Siger
formulated the most profound expression of
medieval scholastic thought. They and their
colleagues on the faculties of arts and
theology made Paris the most celebrated
university throughout western Europe. In the
artistic sphere Notre-Dame became a
towering triumph of the Gothic style. Rarely
in the annals of intellectual and artistic
history does such cultural brilliance occur in
such limited time and space. The Paris of
King Louis IX along with the Athens of
Pericles, the Rome of Augustus, and later the

THE POLITICAL PROLOGUE

Florence of the Medicis are likewise outstanding examples of this achievement.

Since Louis IX was partial to the friars, especially to the Franciscan and Dominican orders, Bonaventure and Thomas Aquinas were personally acquainted with the king and occasionally enjoyed the bounty of his table. But individual favoritism and patronage were not Louis' chief contributions to the cultural brilliance of Paris in the thirteenth century; rather, as king his primary service was political. What then was Louis' part in making Paris the intellectual and artistic center of the medieval world? What are the political prerequisites of culture? Medieval governments attempted to provide justice and soldiers: justice which comprised a legal system to supervise men's social relations and soldiers to police the courts' decisions from within and to guard the subjects from without. Lacking a minimum of regulation and protection, schools cannot function and artists cannot create. Perhaps more than any facet of civilized society, cultural achievement requires a modicum of political stability. We shall see that throughout the Middle Ages this basic condition was secured only with great difficulty. Even as late as the thirteenth century much of western Europe did not enjoy the essentials of orderly society. Alexander of Hales was born in Shropshire, England, one of the Welsh Marches where border fighting was endemic. Albert the Great was a son of the Swabian counts of Bollstädt who witnessed the political deterioration of Germany after the death of the Emperor Henry VI in 1197. Bonaventure came from the small town of Bagnorea near Orvieto in the papal estates where the pope was never strong enough to master the political situation. And Thomas Aquinas was a son of the counts of Aquino in the "Land of Travail" lying to the south of Rome whose peace was constantly threatened by the conflicts between the popes and emperors.

By contrast, the domains of the French king enjoyed tranquility and order uncommon for their day. In 1259, two years after Bonaventure and Thomas became professors, Louis negotiated a treaty which redefined English and French possessions and removed a major source of contention between the two kings. The political calm that was secured in the royal lands by the mid-thirteenth century can perhaps be best illustrated by the history of the castle of Montlhéri. Situated on the direct route between Paris and Orléans, this castle was used by petty barons to disrupt communications between the two chief towns of the royal domain. By a stroke of luck, King Philip I was able to take possession of the stronghold at the turn of the eleventh century. "Look son," he advised the future Louis VI, "make sure you never let the tower of Montlhéri out of your keeping. It has caused me untold trouble. Frankly that tower has made me old before my time." A century and half later King Louis IX found occasion—perhaps it was one of the dinners at which

Bonaventure and Thomas were present—to recount an anecdote about a famous theologian who was troubled with doubts over the holy eucharist. In this story the castle of La Rochelle, which bore the brunt of the English attack in Poitou, served to symbolize the theologian besieged with disbelief, while the castle of Montlhéri "in the heart of France and a land of peace," as Louis phrased it, stood for the political stability of the French kingdom.

To appreciate the magnitude of this achievement requires a brief look at the political experience of medieval Europe. At the opening of the Christian era the Roman Empire provided political order for the Mediterranean lands. From the triumph of Augustus (31 B.C.) to the death of Marcus Aurelius (A.D. 180), never had Europeans enjoyed such long and undisturbed peace. But internal flaws began to appear in the third century, and barbarians pressed upon the borders in the fourth. Attracted by the brilliance and durability of Roman civilization, German tribes migrated *en masse* into the western provinces. Hoping to perpetuate the Roman order, they precipitated the collapse of imperial administration in the West. One of the Germanic tribes, the Franks, strove to unite the heartland of Europe under a stable government in the eighth and ninth centuries. Reviving the imperial ideal of Rome, Charles the Great attempted to create a continental state by sheer force of military skill and personal energy. Suffering from serious internal weaknesses and buffeted with renewed attacks by Slavs, Saracens, and Vikings from without, the Carolingian Empire, as it was called, could not long outlast the death of its founder. By the end of the ninth century, Europe was plunged into political confusion that might truly be called the "Dark Ages" of western civilization. With the disintegration of central government, local communities were forced to rely on their own resources to provide the essentials of regulation and protection. Thus emerged the political pattern known as feudalism, which is best associated with the appearance of castles. He who commanded the castle could terrorize the immediate countryside into accepting his leadership and protection. He thereby controlled the processes of justice and provided the chief defense of the region. Since his authority extended only as far as his military effectiveness—usually the distance over which he could make a sortie from his castle and return to safety—the feudal regime was condemned to local control and endemic warfare. From the disappearance of the Roman Empire, therefore, western Europe's primary prerequisite was a central authority strong enough to provide political stability for a large realm.

The medieval heirs to the Roman title of emperor and aspirations to universal rule were the Germans. After Charlemagne had reinstated the office of Roman emperor, it was transmitted to his successors in the eastern part of his empire and eventually to the Saxon and Salian dynasties that followed them. During the subsequent Hohenstaufen dynasty of the mid-twelfth century, Frederick Barbarossa added the designation "holy" to the Roman title. Although the Hohenstaufens claimed authority over all other kings in Latin Christendom, their pretensions were never realized in practice. In fact the Holy Roman Emperors were no more than the Kings of the Germans throughout the Middle Ages, who occasionally exercised an unstable rule over northern Italy.

The confusion which followed Charlemagne's death in the ninth century affected all of the Carolingian Empire, but it was not as severe in the East. The Saxon and Salian successors, therefore, attempted to perpetuate the Carolingian forms of government in the tenth and eleventh centuries, but they introduced one important change. To strengthen their position they confided preponderant administrative and military responsibility to the bishops of their lands, which in turn required that these churchmen be chosen exclusively by imperial appointment. During the tenth and early eleventh centuries this imperial-episcopal alliance worked remarkably well in subduing the chaotic tendencies of the local nobility, and Germany was undoubtedly the best-governed realm in western Europe. In the second half of the eleventh century, however, a party of church reformers wished to abolish the imperial control over episcopal appointments. When this reform was championed by Pope Gregory VII, an open contest, known as the Investiture Conflict, broke out between the emperor and the Papacy. The result was civil war in Germany in which the local aristocracy were the eventual victors. By the early twelfth century, feudalism with its attendant proliferation of castles appeared on the German scene.

In the mid-twelfth century Frederick Barbarossa of the Hohenstaufen dynasty made another concerted effort to strengthen imperial authority in Germany by regularizing and subordinating the feudal elements under the emperor's leadership. More important, he reinforced the Hohenstaufen ancestral lands in Swabia by marrying the heiress of Burgundy to the west and by intervening in Italian affairs to the south. These policies were successfully continued by his son Henry VI, especially the imperial penetration into Italy, when Henry married Constance, the heiress of southern Italy and Sicily. But once again the imperial hopes were cut short, this time by Henry's sudden death in 1197 which left a three-year-old son, Frederick, as successor. Germany was again consumed by civil war between rival contenders encouraged by France and England, and most important, the Papacy. The popes were alarmed by the imperial interventions in northern Italy and by the recent acquisition of southern Italy which threatened to encircle them. By pitting one party against another, Pope Innocent III (1198–1216) methodically destroyed the bases of imperial authority in Germany. When the young Frederick II was finally crowned emperor in the early thirteenth century, the imperial plans for north of the Alps were abandoned and he became totally absorbed in Sicilian affairs. When he died in 1250 without legitimate successor, three imperial dynasties had failed to secure political continuity and sufficient landed strength to rule Germany and Italy effectively. The Roman imperial dream vanished before the reality of princely warfare and anarchy.

At the turn of the tenth century, however, the aspirations and achievements of the Saxon dynasty encouraged a cultural awakening. The court of the emperor Otto III, for example, attracted Gerbert of Aurillac, the foremost authority in mathematics and science of his day, and Bernwald, Bishop of Hildesheim, who made his bishopric a brilliant artistic center, known especially for manuscript illumination, gold work, bronze sculptures and architecture. But this "Ottonian Renaissance," as it is sometimes called, did not outlast the Investiture struggle of the eleventh century. By the following century German students sought learning in France and Italy and no university appeared in imperial lands until the middle of the fourteenth century, all of which is mute testimony to the political confusion of Germany's medieval past.

In the city of Rome itself the medieval heir to imperial authority was the pope. When the emperors abandoned the city and imperial administration collapsed in the West in the fifth century, the only figure capable of filling the political vacuum was the bishop of Rome. Consequently the popes negotiated with the barbarians and governed the city in the early Middle Ages. To strengthen their authority, the Carolingian emperors made donations of lands in central Italy, which were subsequently known as the Papal States. Although the popes intended to govern these lands like any political ruler, in fact, they exercised little authority until the time of Innocent III, when the confusion which followed Henry VI's death allowed the Papacy to profit again from the political vacuum. In the second half of the thirteenth century, the acquisition of the Romagna, including the important city of Bologna, extended papal territories in a diagonal band across the central Italian peninsula. Beginning with Innocent III, the popes attempted to build an administration based on local rectors, treasurers, judges, and travelling inspectors, but the enemies of effective government were too numerous. The quarrelsome citizens of Rome, the independent communes, the bellicose nobility, and the great families which contended to place their candidates on the papal throne, all defended their local interests against papal authority. When the German emperors began to intervene in Italian affairs, the popes were forced to ally with the Norman kings of Sicily to counterbalance their influence. When the Hohenstaufen emperors acquired Sicily itself, the popes reacted desperately against this imperial encirclement.

The total effect of these forces was virtually to frustrate the efforts of popes to build a strong government over their lands in the twelfth and thirteenth centuries. In a letter written during one of the brighter periods even Innocent III deplored the "dissensions and wars . . . devastations of towns, destructions of castles, burning of villages, oppression of the poor, persecution of churches, men slain and made captive, injuries, violence and rapine." The popes were rarely allowed to reside long at Rome. Most of their business was conducted from Tusculum, Orvieto, Spoleto, or Benevento, an enclave deep in Norman territory. Although the popes hoped to secure money and soldiers from their landed domain like other medieval rulers, they found their estates virtually unmanageable and unproductive of financial and military assistance.

If the medieval popes were political failures at home, they nonetheless succeeded in making their influence felt throughout Latin Christendom even in political matters. We have seen that in the eleventh century reforming popes intervened in imperial affairs to free the church from secular control. In the course of the Investiture Conflict, Pope Gregory VII formally deposed the Emperor Henry IV and released his subjects from their obedience. By the end of the century the Papacy initiated the crusading movement against the Muslims which called on the European rulers throughout the twelfth and thirteenth centuries. In the mid-twelfth century Pope Alexander III, faced with opposition and schism in Italy, went into exile in France and lent his support and prestige to the French king, Louis VII. Pope Innocent III excommunicated King John of England and placed his kingdom under interdict to force him to accept the papal candidate for the Archbishopric of Canterbury. Similar coercion was applied to King Philip Augustus of France to make him take back his estranged wife, and we remember that Innocent III intervened in the disputed contest over the German emperorship. During the thirteenth century the popes enlisted widespread aid in their struggle against the Hohenstaufens.

As the popes extended their influence throughout western Europe, they developed administrative organs within their central court. They perfected a chancery to handle correspondence and a *camera* to receive finances. Papal legates with full authority to enact the pope's commands and resolve local disputes were dispatched throughout Christendom. Most important, a system of ecclesiastical courts was instituted in which appeals could proceed from the local tribunals finally to the papal *curia*. As the head of the church, the pope was the highest judge of Christendom and his decisions pronounced in the *curia* became the supreme law of the church. Because of these legal responsibilities, the cardinals increasingly chose popes who were trained in law. Pope Alexander III was both a student and a professor of law at Bologna before his election and Innocent

III likewise had studied law at Bologna. During the thirteenth century their example was followed by popes such as Gregory IX, Innocent IV and Boniface VIII. As former students and professors of law and now as active judges, these popes were naturally concerned with legal codification and the development of canonistic jurisprudence. Innocent III issued the first official collection of papal decisions for use in the courts and schools. Gregory IX promulgated the definitive collection in 1234, known as the *Decretales,* to which Boniface VIII added a new section at the end of the century. To study these decretals and formulate a science of jurisprudence the popes encouraged and patronized Romanists and canonists at Bologna.

Expert in the law and inclined to intervene in political affairs throughout western Europe, the popes required formulation of their political authority. Gregory VII's deposing of Henry IV implied that the popes exercised jurisdiction over emperors and kings. When Innocent III supported one candidate and then another to the imperial throne, he claimed the right to judge their qualifications for office. While these actions may have suggested that the pope exercised supreme and universal political authority, Innocent hesitated to express this claim without ambiguity. At the middle of the thirteenth century, however, Pope Innocent IV declared without qualification that the pope possessed universal temporal authority, and by the end of the century Boniface VIII decreed that all Christians owed final obedience to the pope in political as well as religious matters. Thus in theory the popes of the thirteenth century conceived of themselves as universal monarchs governing the world. As the popes' claims became more extreme, the gap between theory and practice became more apparent. Insecure in their Italian possessions, and threatened by imperial encirclement, the popes lacked the political means to implement their dreams of universal papal monarchy. When they clashed with the national kingdoms of France and England at the end of the thirteenth century, as we shall see, they were helpless before the coercive powers of the monarchy. The result was their subjugation to French influence and the removal of their court from Italy to Avignon just outside the borders of France. The Avignon exile was a rude awakening from the Roman dream.

While the emperors and popes were unable to provide political stability for their subjects, the kings of England and France took the first steps towards this goal in the twelfth and thirteenth centuries. When William, Duke of Normandy, successfully invaded England and acquired the English crown, he and his followers brought with them the military and political institutions to which they were accustomed in France. In one stroke William superimposed a feudal regime on England in which political jurisdiction as well as land was distributed among the barons. Once again the appearance of castles marked the feudalization of another realm. But the Anglo-Saxon kingdom which William acquired offered him several advantages not found on the Continent. Isolated from the mainland, England had survived the Viking invasions with more peace and security than the Carolingian Empire. From his Anglo-Saxon predecessors William inherited a national administrative system of shires, a national tax based on land, and an obligation for all free men to swear an oath of fealty to the king. These political devices, which pertained to all the free inhabitants of the island, strengthened royal government.

During the next two centuries the English kings exploited to their advantage the process of centralization initiated by the Anglo-Saxons. The shire system was retained and royal agents always played an important role in local affairs. To meet the ever increasing demands for money, new forms of national revenue based on land and moveable property were derived from the former Anglo-Saxon tax. From the central royal court the monarchs created governmental bureaus which specialized in essential political functions. A chancery was perfected for correspondence; an exchequer was devised to handle finances with its own system of accounting and records. Most important, King Henry II (1154–1189) organized a system of royal courts which extended the king's law (known as common law) throughout the realm. Itinerant justices who heard appeals to the royal courts circulated throughout the kingdom. Since the king's justice was more efficient and speedy, it competed successfully with the feudal courts of the barons. Moreover, by the thirteenth century the kings created a representative body, eventually known as parliament, which enabled them to secure consent to new taxes and enlist public opinion on behalf of their policies. Still, every attempt by royal authority to strengthen the functions of central government was resisted by the barons who defended their local interests. The course of English history during the twelfth and thirteenth centuries followed a two-phased rhythm of royal action and baronial reaction. King John's policies, for example, provoked the baronial rebellion which led to Magna Carta in 1215, and later King Henry III's administration incited the uprising of barons under the leadership of Simon of Monfort.

Despite the baronial reactions, England was comparatively well ruled and enjoyed considerable peace in the thirteenth century. To govern a small, compact island of less than four million inhabitants requires less skill than to rule a large, sprawling territory with many times the population on the Continent. When Henry II came to the throne in 1154, he inherited not only England and Normandy from his mother, but also Anjou, Maine and Touraine from his father. His marriage to Eleanor brought Aquitaine as well under

English control. This Angevin Empire, comprising lands many times the size of England, stretched from the Channel to the Pyrenees and included most of western France. Without benefit of an Anglo-Saxon tradition of central monarchy and forced to rely on the existing feudal regime, the English kings were not nearly as successful in governing their Continental domain. We shall see that by the beginning of the thirteenth century they lost all but the southwest part to the French kings. Nonetheless, the English monarchs were able to implant their governmental institutions in Normandy, so that when the French acquired the duchy they had a new political model to follow. In many respects the Angevin kings of England were the schoolmasters of the Capetian kings of France in the thirteenth century.

More than any other region in Europe, the French lands suffered from the dissolution of the Carolingian Empire in the ninth century. Governmental functions were dispersed among countless local lords whose authority extended no further than the immediate vicinity of their castles. A new royal dynasty named the Capetians, who succeeded the Carolingians in France in the tenth century, were kings in title only; they had virtually no influence outside of their ancestral domain, the Ile-de-France, a tiny territory centered on Paris and Orléans. During the first half of the twelfth century, however, the lords of larger fiefs in northern France, such as Flanders, Anjou, and Champagne, began to lay siege to the castles of their petty vassals and to concentrate political and military authority in their own hands. The Capetian kings also participated in this movement of consolidation. By suppressing turbulent noblemen and acquiring strategic castles, such as Montlhéri, they succeeded in putting their domain in order where the popes had failed in Italy. Outside of the Ile-de-France, however, they were intimidated by the military strength of neighboring fiefs, and during the second half of the twelfth century, they were confronted by the vast continental holdings of the English kings. Against such obstacles, caution and patience were the only policies available to the French monarchy in the twelfth century.

A strong and effective government was not achieved in France until the thirteenth century, and then it was largely due to the efforts of the three Capetian kings. Philip Augustus (1180–1223) laid the foundations for royal rule at the beginning of the century. Louis IX (1226–1270) firmly established royal authority during his long and peaceful reign, and Philip the Fair (1285–1314) at the end of the century brought the process to a dramatic and successful climax. In one sense it was a strictly dynastic achievement. Not until the beginning of the fourteenth century did the Capetians fail to produce a male heir. No contested successions to the throne plagued the French monarchy with recurring anarchy as they had the German emperors and the English kings. Only once in the thirteenth century—during the minority of Louis IX—was the Capetian inheritance seriously threatened, but the determination of the queen mother coupled with the indecision of the rebellious barons preserved the French crown. With this minor exception, the legitimate authority of the house of Capet remained uncontested throughout the century.

We have seen that during the second half of the twelfth century the most serious challenge to the Capetians in France came from the kings of England. Claiming almost half of France, the English monarchs divided the loyalties of the French feudal nobility. After decades of vacillating rear-guard action, Philip Augustus was the first to take the offensive against the English. Between 1203 and 1205, he wrested the rich province of Normandy from their hands and his resounding victory at the battle of Bouvines (1214) over a combined German and English army assured him possession of northern France. From then on the English were confined to Aquitaine, but they persisted as a nuisance in habitually troubled regions such as Poitou. These gains against the English provided Philip Augustus with the first significant addition to the royal domain. Since he drew most of his revenue from the domainal lands, (i.e. those lands directly under royal control), the acquisition of Normandy probably doubled the royal income. Succeeding kings made smaller accretions, and by the end of the century Philip the Fair arranged for the annexation of two major fiefs, Toulouse and Champagne. Throughout the thirteenth century the Capetians enjoyed land and revenue undreamed of by their forebears.

The rapid expansion of the royal domain required that the king's administration keep apace. The English monarchy and the newly acquired Normandy furnished the most available guidance for strengthening royal government. Influenced by the itinerant justices of Henry II, Philip Augustus created a class of local officials called *baillis* who originally heard lawsuits, but eventually collected revenues and policed the royal lands. Directly appointed by the king and salaried from his treasury, these men were true royal agents, free from feudal obligations. By the time of Louis IX they were not only the chief local official in the domain but also penetrated neighboring fiefs where the local barons were not strong enough to prevent their intervention. The need to coordinate the activities of these officials encouraged the development of centralized organs of administration. Philip Augustus located his archives and established his bureau of audit at Paris. The *parlement* or chief royal law court (not to be confused with the English parliament) was detached from the king's court and established permanently at Paris during the reign of Louis IX. Following the example of the English parliament, Philip the Fair summoned a representative body, known as the

Estates General, composed of the major classes of the kingdom to enlist support against the Papacy, the English and other foes. These governmental organs—local as well as central—were increasingly staffed with men trained in Roman law. This efficient bureaucracy helped to establish a stable and effective government for France.

A visible indication of the Capetian triumph may be found in the transformation of Paris into the royal capital. Among the cities of the Ile-de-France Paris was probably chosen by the Capetians because of its proximity to the Norman border where military operations against the English could be directed and because of its nearby forests celebrated for their excellent hunting. Also close to the city was the royal abbey of Saint-Denis where the sacred relics of the patron saint of France were treasured. Along with the geographic advantages, these symbolic traditions weighed heavily in the minds of the Capetians when they made Paris the administrative center of the kingdom. Philip Augustus inclosed it with a wall, paved its principal streets, introduced aqueducts, and constructed a market place. Philip the Fair rebuilt the royal palace in magnificent proportions. Paris, the largest city of northern Europe, expressed the full measure of the Capetian aspirations.

The French achievement of the thirteenth century benefited substantially from the cooperation of the church. When Clovis, king of the Franks, was baptized into the Catholic faith in the fifth century, he distinguished his people from the other Germanic tribes which had adopted heretical forms of Christianity. The orthodoxy of the Frankish rulers, therefore, encouraged a policy of close collaboration with the popes. As heirs to this Frankish tradition, the Capetians became known as the favorite sons of the Roman church. When Pope Urban II preached the First Crusade, it was to France he came to enlist recruits. When Alexander III fled Italy from his enemies, he sought refuge with the Capetians and sent the French King Louis VII, also in trouble at home, a golden rose as an emblem of his esteem. King Louis IX was always ready to respond to a papal summons for a crusade. Unlike the emperors or even the English kings, the Capetians were seldom in serious disagreement with the popes until the end of the thirteenth century. As a corollary of this French-papal accord, French churchmen actively supported the Capetian program. Suger, Abbot of Saint-Denis, served as chief lieutenant to two kings in the early twelfth century. In contrast to the German episcopacy after the Investiture Conflict, most French bishops rendered loyal aid and counsel to the monarchy. Louis IX, as we have seen, was favorably disposed to the friars and often employed them in royal administration. The Capetian crown in many respects rested securely on a clerical miter.

During his long reign King Louis IX witnessed the culmination of medieval French culture. His contribution to this achievement was a remarkable charisma which inspired loyalty and devotion among his subjects. The characteristic which most impressed his contemporaries was his genuine piety. Louis had a way of expressing pure motives and personal sanctity that went far beyond customary devotion. He was the one crusader of the thirteenth century whose sincerity could not be impugned and whose death therefore carried an authentic aura of martyrdom. By the end of the century when his canonization was accomplished, the Capetians numbered one of their own among the company of the saints. But Louis' personal appeal was not limited to religion. Regarding the sins of his realm as his own responsibility, he demonstrated an overriding passion to eradicate injustice. After hearing reports of extortion by local royal officials, he commissioned investigators throughout the domain to hear complaints and rectify abuses. And it was not merely a moral compulsion which stirred the king, because during his reign the system of royal courts was perfected. Louis' solicitude for justice was most vividly captured by his biographer when he pictured the king seated under an oak at Vincennes outside of Paris, imparting justice to all who would come.

Louis' gifts to France included peace as well as prestige, and his devotion to the cause of peace was more than conventional. He made realistic settlements with Aragon and England that eased serious points of contention. The king of England and his rebellious barons accepted him as a trustworthy arbitrator of their differences. He refused to profit from the wars between the Hohenstaufens and the Papacy, and within France he took measures to restrain the feuding habits of the nobility by finding peaceful solutions to baronial quarrels. He also restricted judicial duels and the carrying of arms, so that it was increasingly difficult and unprofitable to indulge in private warfare within the royal domain. Even if his measures were not always successful, Louis' reign did bestow on France an unprecedented era of harmony which encouraged economic prosperity and flourishing culture. The France of Saint Louis was the cradle of scholastic thought and Gothic art, both of which represented the highest cultural achievements of the Middle Ages. Not until the seventeenth century under Louis XIV would French culture again dominate the civilization of Europe.

Strength at home naturally led to influence abroad. As a result of the growing French prestige, the cardinals elected four Frenchmen to the papal throne during the second half of the thirteenth century. One of these, Urban IV, attempted to improve the papal position in Italy by offering the crown of Sicily to Charles of Anjou, the younger brother of Louis IX. Although Louis himself had resisted the temptation to intervene beyond the French borders for his own profit, he consented to the adventure. Charles accepted and the French were increasingly involved in Mediterranean affairs for centuries to come. Not only did French culture dominate western Europe, but French kings also assumed greater responsibility in international affairs.

The practical achievements of the kings of France and England eventually had to be squared with the theoretical claims of the papal monarchy. Could the popes persuade these successful rulers to accept their authority in temporal affairs? When Boniface VIII in the name of papal supremacy forbade Philip the Fair of France and Edward I of England to tax the clergy without his permission, he provoked a direct confrontation between the spiritual and temporal powers. During the resulting conflict the bureaucratic agents of Philip mounted a propaganda campaign against the pope's integrity and organized a party to kidnap him bodily. When the shock of this unparalleled outrage precipitated the death of the aged Boniface, the cardinals recognized the superiority of brute force by electing a Frenchman. The succeeding French popes institutionalized the political realities by moving the papal court from Italy to Avignon outside the French border. The old cooperation between the Capetians and Papacy dissolved into increased domination over the pope by the French king. The Avignese Papacy, which lasted for over seventy years (1305–1378), was followed by a great schism (1378–1409) when efforts were made to bring the pope back to Rome. Thus two lines of popes, one Roman, the other French, completed the degradation of the Papacy as the independent and undisputed leader of Latin Christendom. While these evils befell the church, the monarchs of France and England were engaged in the Hundred Years' War, which devasted the French countryside during the fourteenth and fifteenth centuries. And, as if these political ills were not sufficient, western Europe was visited with the Black Plague, unprecedented famine, and catastrophic decline in population. To Frenchmen of the fourteenth and fifteenth centuries tormented by war, sickness, hunger, and death, the thirteenth century, "the good old days of Saint Louis," could not help but appear as a golden age.

The Countryside

As the year 1003 approached, people all over the world, but especially in Italy and France began to rebuild their churches. Although most of them were well built and in little need of alterations, Christian nations were rivalling each other to have the most beautiful edifices. One might say the world was shaking herself, throwing off her old garments, and robing herself with a white mantle of churches. Then nearly all the cathedrals, the monasteries dedicated to different saints, and even the small village chapels were reconstructed more beautifully by the faithful.[1]

In this well-known passage the Burgundian chronicler Ralph Glaber evokes a new age heralded by the reconstruction and multiplication of stone churches. To the modern historian, the rise of church building is a sure indication of an increase in the number of the faithful. From the beginning of the eleventh century, when Ralph Glaber wrote, through the end of the thirteenth, the population of western Europe rose steeply. Norman England possessed 1,100,000 inhabitants in 1086 and 3,700,000 in 1346. Although exact figures are not easily found for the Continent, there is no doubt that the population at least doubled during the same period, with the sharpest rise occurring around the year 1200. This phenomenal demographic expansion continued until the beginning of the fourteenth century when the catastrophes of famine, plague and war decimated millions. In 1377, the English population dropped to 2,200,000 and most countries did not regain their former levels until the sixteenth century. Throughout the twelfth and thirteenth centuries, however, western Europeans were reproducing themselves at an accelerated rate.

Since the overwhelming proportion of medieval population lived in the countryside,

THE URBAN SETTING

[1]Raoul Glaber, *Les cinq livres de ses histoires*, ed. Maurice Prou (Paris, 1886), p. 62.

Oxford o Cambridge
o
   London

Arras • Ghent
      • Douai
      + Amiens
Bec o ō Laon ō
Paris ō   o Reims
Chartres ō
Orléans o   ō Sens   + Strasbourg
          CHAMPAGNE

                • Milan   Venice
                          o Padua
          Genoa Po R.
Montpellier o   o Bologna
          Pisa •   • Florence

                    • Rome
o Toledo

                    o Salerno

o Schools
+ Gothic Cathedrals
ō Schools and Gothic Cathedrals
--- Land trade route

this demographic revolution was closely related to an accompanying agricultural revolution. The increase of people is most clearly seen in the extension of arable land. Before 1000, western Europe was largely blanketed with forests and wastelands, but by 1300 more trees had been felled, more swamps drained, more soil turned by the plow than ever before. Peasants and lords alike shared the prodigious task of reclaiming the soil for agriculture. As early as the eleventh century peasants were enlarging the clearings around their villages on their own initiative. By the second half of the twelfth century the lords recognized the profit in extending the area of cultivation and began to encourage projects of colonization. New villages (*villeneuves*) were founded in the wilderness, which attracted pioneer inhabitants (*hôtes*) through favorable privileges and liberties. Eventually, the best lands were claimed for the plough, so that by the end of the thirteenth century the lack of fertile soil brought about a decrease in land exploitation. The external conquest of soil was succeeded by an internal effort enabling farmers to cultivate their fields more intensively. Crop yields were increased by the rotation of crops, the close regulation of fallow land in the three-field system, and the application of manure. Moreover, the improvement of tools, such as the iron plough, and the introduction of draught horses made more effective by collar harnesses raised the efficiency of human labor expended on the land. The ploughman with his team of horses, many times more efficient than a gang of manual laborers, became the new figure of the agricultural revolution. Extensive cultivation and improvement of agricultural techniques therefore kept the food supply abreast of the population increase.

During the early Middle Ages agriculture was orientated towards the self-sufficient manor. In this local community the peasants produced the necessities for themselves and their lord and very little else. We shall see, however, that trading activity and town life also revived in the eleventh century, which had profound effects on the countryside as well. Chief among these was the introduction of the money economy into rural life. Produce could now be exchanged for currency, and crops could be sold on more distant markets. Since bread was the chief staple of medieval diet, grain remained the primary crop of western Europe, but now it could be produced at a price for more distant consumers living in towns. Although variable local conditions caused the grain price to fluctuate violently over short terms, the long-range price continued to rise because of the continuous demand generated by population expansion. While grain remained a profitable crop, the more distant consumer encouraged the landholder to consider other products. The changing tastes and growing affluence of nobility and townsmen demanded better grades of wine which could be produced in certain French regions. Similarly, the demand for more luxurious woolen cloth encouraged urban weavers. The demands of the wool industry along with the need of parchment for books and meat for the table stimulated the raising of sheep on a large scale. This increase of the vineyard and the sheep pasturage are just two examples of the town's and commerce's influence on the countryside.

Landholders no longer limited production to their immediate needs, but began to organize their demesnes for crops which could be profitably sold on the market. Improved techniques for breeding sheep were introduced to increase the wool yield. Highly skilled labor was required to dress the vines and to gather the grapes. Literate clerks were needed to keep records and accounts to manage the estates more rationally. Organization, specialization, and professionalization transformed the autonomous manor into a business enterprise. The labor services which the lord formerly exacted from his unfree peasants were no longer sufficiently skilled or efficient to serve the new demesne farming. Now that crops were fetching prices, money could be used to hire trained help. Throughout the twelfth and especially the thirteenth century, peasant labor services and personal servitudes were increasingly commuted into money.

Unneeded land was frequently leased for cash rents. With this extra money landlords employed their peasants as day laborers at an agreed wage. While the growing population helped to augment the price of grain, it also tended to keep wages stable. By the second half of the thirteenth century there appeared definite signs that the countryside was overpopulated, thus assuring the lord of an abundant supply of cheap labor. Although the population increase supported the landholder's prosperity, the accompanying money economy secured certain advantages to the peasant as well. Free from labor services and personal servitudes and supported by wages, he possessed greater flexibility to move about for his personal advantage. The skilled ploughman could now command a wage commensurate with his efficiency. Some peasants achieved sufficient prosperity to enfranchise themselves completely and enter the ranks of free landholders. Other rich peasants, particularly in southern France and Italy, penetrated the towns and intermarried with the wealthy townsmen and nobility. In all events, a surplus and increasingly mobile population was drawn from the countryside into the towns to provide manual labor for new commerce and industries.

Peasant life varies markedly from region to region, so that it is difficult to draw generalizations valid for the whole of western Europe. Equally characteristic, peasant life changes slowly, almost imperceptibly, so that chronological development is hard to discern. Nonetheless, in two areas, northern Italy and the Ile-de-France, the transformations occurred rapidly and in advance of other lands. For example, labor servitudes first declined in Italy and rents penetrated Italian landholdings at least a century before the rest of Europe. The Ile-de-France was favorable to an early dissemination of *villeneuves* and the three-field system, an advanced technique of crop rotation. Undoubtedly, the agricultural precocity of northern Italy and the Ile-de-France was related to their urban centers. Milan, Genoa, Venice and Paris therefore stimulated the agricultural revolution in the countryside.

The Commercial Revolution

Although the causal relationships are not fully known, it is clear that the demographic and agricultural revolutions were closely connected. Neither is there any doubt that they were intimately involved in a third concurrent movement—the commercial revolution, which revived urban civilization in western Europe. The localized, self-sufficient, stagnant economy of the early Middle Ages allowed little place for commerce, but in the eleventh century when the population began to increase and agriculture began to expand, trading activity also began to accelerate. It rose sharply until the beginning of the fourteenth century when it levelled off in some areas and declined in others. Long distance commerce was concentrated in two major areas, first a southern trade zone centered on the Mediterranean and later a northern area centered on the North Sea. While sea transport was most efficient for these two zones, land routes were eventually established to link them. The most travelled one led up the Rhone valley, across the plains of Champagne, then turned northeast to Flanders. At the beginning long-distance trade consisted largely of expensive luxury items which could be easily transported—spices, fine cloth and wine—while later, merchant cargos also included grain, lumber, and salt.

The commercial revolution produced not only a sharply rising volume of trade, but also improvements in business techniques. In this latter realm, the merchants of northern Italy were the true innovators and devised commercial practices which were later adopted throughout the rest of western Europe. In the early stages the merchant usually accompanied his wares and bargained directly with sellers and buyers. Fairs provided convenient meeting places for these travelling merchants. For example, halfway along the overland route between the Mediterranean and the North Sea the Italian merchants met their Flemish counterparts at the famous fairs of Champagne where they exchanged cloth, leather and other wares. To finance his ventures, the Italian trader formed simple partnerships with investors in which one member supplied the capital, another the labor (and perhaps part of the capital too), and the risks of the affair were shared proportionately. Gradually, however, the Italian men of business devised methods which allowed them to remain at home and conduct more widespread affairs through agents. By means of business correspondence, bookkeeping procedures, insurance, letters of credit, bills of exchange, banking facilities and other commercial devices, they ushered in the modern age of business practice. The decline of the fairs of Champagne at the turn of the thirteenth century indicated that the new sedentary merchant was replacing his itinerant predecessor.

Urban Revival

The upswing of commerce, which began in the eleventh century, was accompanied by a revival of town life in western Europe. Simple reflection will reveal that trade and towns are two sides of the same coin. Antithetical to a local, self-sufficient economy, both involve specialization of production and services and their mutual exchange. Neither can succeed without the other. The city had been an integral part of ancient Mediterranean civilization since its origin. The Mesopotamians possessed their urban clusters, the Greeks their *poleis* and the Romans their *civitates*. In the Classical era the concept and the name itself of civilization was intimately related to the city. In the third century A.D., however, the vitality of Classical urban civilization began to decline. The Germanic invasions of the fourth and fifth centuries further undermined city life, but it was the Muslim domination of the Mediterranean in the seventh and eighth centuries that dealt the ancient towns their most serious blow. Although the explanation is complex, a principal factor was the decline in trading acitivity. When, therefore, commercial life reawoke in the eleventh century, towns which had shrunk into the corner of their ancient walls during the hard times of the early Middle Ages began to surpass their original sites and new cities appeared where none formerly existed. Naturally enough, medieval towns displayed greatest vitality where trade was most vigorous. The southern trading zone produced a cluster of cities in northern Italy dominated by Genoa, Pisa, Milan, Florence, and Venice. In the northern area, towns formed in the Flemish lowlands facing England, among which Saint-Omer, Ghent, Douai, Bruges, and Arras were preeminent. In these two clusters urban population achieved maximum density—at least one third of the Flemish lived in towns —but cities also appeared throughout most of western Europe.

Stimulated by the growth in population, agriculture and commerce, townsmen were constantly enlarging their walls to include their burgeoning number of inhabitants. Italy could boast of five or six cities (Milan, Genoa, Venice, Naples, Florence, and Palermo) which exceeded 50,000, and Florence probably attained 100,000 by the beginning of the fourteenth century. In Flanders only Ghent exceeded the 50,000 figure, and the vast majority of European cities numbered only a few thousand. Although medieval towns were not large by modern standards and never comprised more than ten per cent of the total population, they constituted the most rapidly expanding sector of medieval society. The extension of walls and the multiplication of parishes show that in the thirteenth century the town was growing more rapidly than the countryside. This urban vitality was most strikingly expressed in its construction programs. In addition to the new fortifications, townsmen erected municipal buildings crowned with towering belfries. Particularly in northern Europe, civic pride encouraged burghers to rebuild their cathedral, thrusting its spires and vaults higher and higher to outdo the efforts of their neighbors. Like the countryside, however, this ebullience could not survive the disasters of pestilence, famine and warfare of the fourteenth century. Florence, for example, saw its population cut in half after the Black Death, and it did not regain its former size for centuries. Other cities never recovered from the misfortunes of the late Middle Ages. Still, the urban prosperity of the thirteenth century furnished the economic basis for the intellectual and artistic achievements of that age. Great universities and

Gothic edifices were the creations of medieval towns. They could feed and lodge thousands of professors and students; they could afford expensive art and monumental architecture.

Medieval towns, like castles and fiefs, exhibited widely diverse characteristics, and nowhere was this particularism more evident than in their forms of government. The cities of greatest consequence, however, may be grouped in two categories according to their Roman origins: those in the Mediterranean basin, particularly in Italy, which were descended from Roman cities without an interruption of urban tradition, and those in the Rhine and Danube valleys and particularly in northern France, which originated as Roman towns but in which the ancient traditions had all but disappeared. The administration of the ancient Roman Empire was based on the city, and the ruling classes of each province made their homes in the imperial cities. The Christian church likewise followed the Roman example by patterning its administration on the cities. Each *civitas* was the seat of the bishop and each important city was the center for an archbishop or metropolitan. In the Mediterranean region where trade was never completely extinguished, these urban traditions of Rome and the church continued. Following the pattern of Classical life, the Italian nobility more often chose to live in town, so that the skyline of an Italian town, in contrast to that of a northern city, was punctuated with tall defensive towers belonging to the prominent families of the region. "Everyone possesses a house with a tower," wrote one twelfth-century Genoese observer, "and when war breaks out the terraces of the towers become fields of battle." With the possible exception of Rome, where the pope occasionally secured political supremacy, control over the government of the Mediterranean cities was sought both by the urban nobility and the bishops.

The situation was different in northern France where trade fell more sharply and urban life disappeared almost totally in the early Middle Ages. The towns were gradually abandoned by the Roman governors, and the new leaders of feudal society avoided the cities, preferring to remain in their castles and country estates. The bishops, however, were required by canon law to remain in their cities. The political vacuum caused by the withdrawal of imperial government and the absence of the feudal aristocracy forced many bishops to assume responsibility for governing the cities. When urban life revived in the eleventh century, many towns were firmly controlled by bishops who considered political jurisdiction part of their ecclesiastical patrimony. In these northern cities it was the bishop, not the nobility, who possessed the castle and manned the walls.

As the towns attracted more people within their walls, these new inhabitants sought a greater voice in their own affairs. They objected to taxes which brought no services, laws which ignored their interests, and wars which jeopardized their prosperity. This conflict of interest between townsmen and their rulers gave rise to a peculiar type of urban government, the town commune. Essentially a commune consisted of an association of men sworn to accomplish a particular purpose—often to overthrow the existing ruler and substitute in his place a collective government of officials elected by the association. The communal movement originated in the eleventh century in northern Italy where both the nobility and the ordinary inhabitants participated, then spread to southern France, and by the twelfth century penetrated northern France. There the target of the revolutionary movement was invariably the bishop, who was fiercely opposed by his townsmen. In the beginning, the communes possessed the characteristic organs of an ancient sovereign state: a popular assembly, a restricted council, and executive power. Eventually, the assembly declined in effectiveness, and the real authority was exercised by the council or the executive power. By the thirteenth century cliques of noble families in Italy or rich patrician merchants in northern France directed the city's affairs by controlling the council. Other Italian cities called in a foreigner to be their *podestà* or city manager in an effort to find an impartial solution to their internal conflicts. Although the communes were initially founded on broad and popular bases, by the end of the thirteenth century they were transformed into oligarchies from which the majority of town dwellers was excluded. In the last analysis their success in self-government depended on the weakness of the king in whose territory they were located. In Italy and Germany where the emperor's government was virtually ineffectual, town communes enjoyed considerable political autonomy, but in France and especially in England where royal administration was well developed, the towns gained little self-rule. Bologna, for example, possessed a long history of communal rule, but the French king never allowed the bourgeoisie of Paris similar political authority.

In Latin terminology the medieval commune was usually called *communio, societas* or *universitas,* which generally meant a collective body of people operating as a single person. A legal corporation is the closest modern equivalent. But the last two terms were applicable to economic as well as political organization. Even before the appearance of communes, *societas* and especially *universitas* had served to designate the medieval guild, which was fundamentally the corporate organization of an economic activity. The simplest form was the merchant guild, which sought to promote the interests of a large comprehensive group of traders without special concern for particular goods or skills. Alongside the merchant guild more specialized craft guilds were formed which represented the concerns of particular trades or industries such as money changing or wool weaving. Some craft guilds appeared in Italy early in the eleventh century, but in northern Europe the merchant guilds came first and specialization only resulted with the maturing of economic life. Paris by the mid-thirteenth century, for example, claimed over a hundred guilds organizing the most minute forms of commerce and industry.

In principle, guilds attempted to regulate the activities of their trade for their members' mutual benefit. Eventually, the successful long distance traders, who originally organized the merchant guilds, had less need for the guild's protection. Capable of expanding their enterprises indefinitely, they began to resent any restrictive measures against their affairs. But the small traders and craftsmen who were limited by the scope of manual labor and who could easily be exploited by the merchant capitalist, found it advantageous to form craft guilds for their mutual protection. Although their regulations touched every aspect of their trade—quantity and quality of production, prices, wages, and hours of work—they were most effective in controlling the supply of skilled labor through regulation of membership. Like any corporate body, the guild was vitally concerned with admission to membership. Normally, full rights were conferred on craftsmen called masters, who had demonstrated their skill by producing a masterwork or *chef d'oeuvre*, which was regarded as a kind of final examination. Not only was attainment of a skill necessary, but the master had also to have an established business which was capable of supporting him. In other words, economic independence as well as maturity qualified one for full membership. Beneath the masters, journeymen (literally day-men) worked for daily wages. They were also known as bachelors because they were not sufficiently established in business themselves and therefore unable to support a family. Since their rights were closely restricted or practically nonexistent, only hope of setting up their own shop and gaining admission into the society of masters kept them within the guild organization. At the bottom of the scale were the apprentices, young boys learning the trade who were maintained and managed by the master. The forms of government within these societies of masters varied widely, but often their leaders bore the title of rector. This organization of economic activity in the guild system would, we shall see, closely correspond to that of intellectual life in the universities of the thirteenth century.

In this brief sketch of medieval towns, we have focused on two primary functions: trade, which furnished economic support, and the varying forms of government, which offered protection and regulation. The topography of a medieval city often displayed these two factors. The political function of protection was situated in a fortified area, generally known in Latin as *burgus*. Often consisting of a castle, it eventually formed the nucleus of the growing town.

Whoever controlled the castle and its fortifications was likely to be the political master of the town. As the city expanded, outlying sections were enclosed within concentric walls, which may be considered as the extension of the *burgus* over the entire community. The suburban dwellings outside the walls were characteristically called *faubourgs* in French, that is, those sections beyond the *burgus.* Eventually these might be included in still another system of fortifications. The commercial function of the town was located in the *portus* or *wik,* which consisted of permanent market places or sections of the city where trade and industry were normally conducted. For protection this mercantile community generally lay close to the *burgus* or was even enclosed with walls. Whenever these two elements of *burgus* and *portus* were combined in a single site, the essential ingredients for a medieval town were present.

Bologna and Paris

Among all the cities which provide the urban setting for the intellectual history of the thirteenth century, by far the most important were Bologna and Paris. Each possessed individual peculiarities and neither can be taken as typical of a medieval town. Still, it was these cities that provided the local environment for the most significant cultural developments of that century. A brief glimpse at their topography will make more vivid the events that happened there.

Bologna belonged to the cluster of cities in northern Italy whose urban life was quickened by the upsurge of Mediterranean trade in the eleventh century. Set in the foothills of the northern slope of the Apennines almost equidistant from both coasts, it faced the Adriatic in the direction of the Po Valley. Although Bologna lacked easy access to either sea, it did enjoy a pivotal position among the land routes of northern Italy. During medieval as well as modern times a large part of the traffic between northern and southern Italy passed through Bologna, making it a center of commerce. Bologna had a long history of communal government, extending back into the tenth century. Since the twelfth, the city had been effectively administered by a single *podestà* who ruled with the advice of councils elected from the citizens. Like many other towns of northern Italy, Bologna was caught in the imperial-papal conflict, and although claimed by both sides, she generally favored the Papacy. In 1249 the city won a spectacular victory against the Emperor Frederick II with the capture of his son, and by 1276 it placed itself formally under the protection of the pope.

The long history of communal government was already apparent in the topography of thirteenth-century Bologna. At the very center of the city stood the Palazzo del Podestà with its imposing tower, which housed the communal government. Toward the end

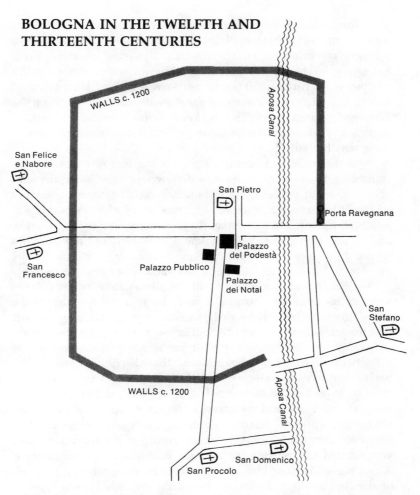

BOLOGNA IN THE TWELFTH AND THIRTEENTH CENTURIES

WALLS c. 1200

Aposa Canal

San Felice e Nabore

San Pietro

Porta Ravegnana

Palazzo del Podestà

San Francesco

Palazzo Pubblico

Palazzo dei Notai

San Stefano

WALLS c. 1200

Aposa Canal

San Domenico

San Procolo

of the century two more communal buildings, the Palazzo Pubblico and the Palazzo dei Notai, were added to form a spacious public square. Although they have been somewhat altered in succeeding centuries, the massive and rough brick facades of these governmental palaces preserve their fortresslike character to this day. The participation of the nobility in Bolognese urban life was indicated by a number of tall but sturdy towers which studded the city and its suburbs. (Two fine examples of these towers, dating from the twelfth century, exist today.) After the tenth century walls surrounding the center of Bologna proved to be hopelessly inadequate, they were enlarged in approximately 1200 to double the size of the city and to allow for a population of about 20,000 inhabitants, but before long even these became obsolete. By the middle of the century the population had perhaps reached 40,000, which would place Bologna among the major cities of medieval Italy.

Communal palaces, the towers of the nobility and the city walls, comprised the *burgus* of Bologna. The *portus* or the commercial section was centered on the municipal market near the Porta Ravegnana to the east of the old walls but well within the thirteenth century walls. Since natural waterways were distant, the citizens of Bologna constructed a system of canals, with water drawn from the Reno and Sareno rivers. The market at Porta Ravegnana benefited particularly from the Aposa Canal, which flowed through the city from north to south.

In the thirteenth century, Bologna was less renowned for its commerce than for its university of law students. Since the university did not possess public buildings at that time, we cannot precisely identify the academic quarters of the city. We do know, however, that professors frequently gave instruction in their houses, and by identifying the parishes where they lived and the churches where they were buried, we can approximate the locations of the university. For example, the canonist Gratian lived at the monastery of San Felice and San Nabore outside the western walls. (It now survives as a military hospital.) Since he was the founder of the study of canon law in the early twelfth century, we may suspect that that subject was taught there. Similarly, Roman law was probably taught in the complex of churches at San Stefano on the east side, because Irnerius, who initiated that discipline early in the twelfth century, was associated with the quarter. Two of Irnerius' most renowned successors were buried at San Procolo in the southern part of the city, and the graves of others are found at the nearby Dominican convent. But the tombs of the most illustrious thirteenth-century professors of Roman law are at the Franciscan convent located just outside the western wall (Plate I). This convent, which was constructed towards the middle of the century, was one of the first attempts to import into Italy the new French style of Gothic architecture. Finally, at the center of Bologna, just to the north of the Palazzo del Podestà, was the cathedral school of San Pietro, where the Archdeacon of Bologna supervised the degrees of the law faculty. Reflecting the general population distribution at Bologna, the quarters of student activity were scattered both within and without the city walls. It is difficult to be precise about educational statistics in the Middle Ages, but we have reason to believe that there were 10,000 students in Bologna in the middle of the thirteenth century. Since the university comprised a significant proportion of the total inhabitants, it undoubtedly contributed to Bologna's expansion over its walls into the surrounding suburbs.

Paris on the river Seine in the heart of the Ile-de-France profited from the northern trade area as well as from its proximity to the overland trade routes through Champagne. The city owed prominence not to its economic position, but to the rising fortunes

I. The tomb of the Glossator Accursius and his son Francesco behind the church of San Francesco in Bologna (*Foto G. Camera, Bologna*)

PARIS IN THE TWELFTH AND THIRTEENTH CENTURIES

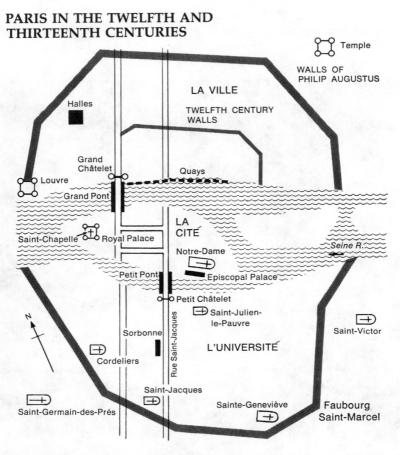

of the Capetian dynasty, who since the twelfth century had designated it as their capital. A large town of about 80,000 inhabitants
in the thirteenth century, Paris bore the marks of a royal city. Never
was a commune with political rights permitted to form because the
city belonged exclusively to the king, who administered it through
a prévôt. Even the bishop of Paris, although the prelate of the
capital, was not allowed the archepiscopal rank. (The nearest archbishop was at Sens.) The original *burgus* was limited to the Ile-
de-la-Cité, the island in the Seine, which was connected to the two
banks by stone bridges defended by small castles known as Châte-
lets. Later the Right Bank or northern portion across from the Cité
was shielded by a wall. By the beginning of the thirteenth century
King Philip Augustus enlarged the scope of these walls and completely encircled the town. At the western point of the fortifications
on the Right Bank he constructed a strong tower called the Louvre.
The king usually resided at the royal palace, which dominated the
western end of the Ile-de-la Cité. Louis IX remodeled parts of it

and constructed the Sainte-Chapelle, an architectural gem of carved stone and stained glass. At the end of the century Philip the Fair added the four great towers on the north side which form the Conciergerie today.

The western part of the Cité was connected with the Right Bank by a bridge lined with shops and known in the thirteenth century as the Grand-Pont or the Pont-au-Change, because these structures were used by goldsmiths and money changers. The Right Bank contained the *portus* or the commercial quarter of Paris. Along the Seine stretched the wharves of the merchants, behind which lay a maze of narrow streets whose names indicated diverse trades and crafts. In this section Philip Augustus constructed the Halles, or the central market, and beyond the walls stood the fortified tower of the Knights Templars, who served as royal bankers.

The eastern part of the Ile-de-la Cité, containing the episcopal palace and the cathedral of Notre-Dame, belonged to the bishop. Begun in 1163 but not completed until the 1270's, this magnificent Gothic edifice was under construction throughout the thirteenth century (Plate II). A cathedral school was held in the cloister of Notre-Dame, and to the north were situated the houses of the clergy. The bishop's portion of the Cité was connected with the Left Bank or the southern section of Paris by the Petit-Pont, which was also surmounted with dwellings, some of which housed schools. The Left Bank, known today as the Latin Quarter, was the university section of town, and was dominated by three collegiate churches served by communities of clerics or monks. To the southwest and outside the walls stood Saint-Germain-des-Prés, a Benedictine abbey, whose stone edifice and tower still stand. Crowning a hill at the southern-most section of the walls was the church of Sainte-Geneviève and southeast of the city lay the church of Saint-Victor. These last two collegiate churches possessed important schools since the twelfth century. Leading south from the Petit-Pont ran the rue Saint-Jacques, so named because it pointed towards the pilgrim shrine of Santiago de Compostela in Spain. Along this street just within the walls the Dominican friars established their convent in 1218, which took its name from the route, and somewhat later the Franciscans occupied another house towards Saint-Germain-des-Près called the Cordeliers. By the end of the thirteenth century the Left Bank was honeycombed with colleges or charitable foundations for students, the most illustrious of which was endowed by Robert of Sorbon, the chaplain to Louis IX, and located just off the rue Saint-Jacques. During the course of the thirteenth century the pressure of 7,000 to 8,000 students, most of whom were concentrated on the Left Bank, soon burst the containing walls, and many were inhabiting *faubourgs* such as that of Saint-Marcel to the south.

By the thirteenth century the island, Right Bank and Left Bank

II. The western façade and towers of Notre-Dame of Paris (*Bildarchiv Foto Marburg 183,447*)

of Paris were popularly designated as *la Cité, la Ville,* and *l'Université.*
It is not insignificant, as we shall see, that the king's half of *la Cité*
was linked by a bridge with the commercial quarter of *la Ville,* and
the bishop's half with *l'Université.*

The Social Structure

The pressure of townsmen which swelled over the walls of Bologna
and Paris was merely one aspect of the long term demographic rise
since the eleventh century. But urban growth was to affect pro-
foundly medieval society in general and learning in particular. City
population expanded more rapidly than the countryside, resulting
in a proportionate increase of urban inhabitants who were no longer
restricted by the customs of rural society. Because the townsman
was involved primarily in commercial activities, he required rights
which were normally denied to the peasants who lived and worked
on the land. He needed personal freedom to do what he wanted,
particularly to travel where he pleased. He needed freedom of
property—to buy, sell, lend, bequeath, and dispose of his goods
as he wished. It was to his great advantage to be released from
burdensome tolls, monopolies, and personal labor duties, all of
which had arisen from an agricultural economy. Finally, he needed
a rational and regular system of law which substituted proof by
witnesses and documents for customary procedures such as ordeals
and judgment by battle. The townsman considered these conditions
prerequisite to the commercial life as his essential liberties, and by
the thirteenth century they were accepted as the normal rights of
all urban dwellers. While cities differed widely in forms of government and political freedom (as Bologna contrasted with Paris), all
townsmen claimed these social and legal liberties as their due. By
contrast to the countryside where the peasant, in spite of the waning
of serfdom, was still subject to numerous restrictions, the town was
an island of social and legal freedom in a sea of seigneurial servitudes. It was the townsman's personal freedom of movement that
was influential on intellectual life. In the early Middle Ages the
scholar dared not venture far beyond the shelter of his monastery
or church. But the new intellectual of the town, following the example of the urban merchant, travelled widely in pursuit of knowledge.
Urban society provided the pattern of mobility necessary for the
dissemination of learning.

The appearance of large bodies of townsmen also produced
revolutionary changes in the organization of medieval society as a
whole. Since the early Middle Ages society was traditionally divided
into three groups: the clergy, the nobility and the peasants. According to a simplistic division of labor, the world consisted therefore
of those who prayed, who fought, and who labored. The first two

were privileged and free; the peasants were not. The urban population, however, presented a significant new class with no fixed place in the traditional scheme. Although townsmen worked like peasants, they also enjoyed privileges and liberties. The cities of western Europe, therefore, dissolved the old tripartite view of society and created a new class called *burgenses*, dwellers of the *burgus*, bourgeoisie, or burghers, which was to outlive the Middle Ages. Moreover, the townsmen further added to the complexity of the medieval scheme of division of labor. Just as craftsmen multiplied their guilds according to their specialized interests, so townsmen began to regard society not in terms of three simple orders but according to numerous specialized professions. We shall see that the urban scholar, following this pattern, began to conceive of himself as an intellectual artisan and his school as his shop. The specialization and professionalization of urban society, therefore, provided a new place and justification for intellectual activity.

The appearance of the bourgeoisie also provided an important impetus for education. In the church's view the term *clericus* or clergyman implied the ability to read and write. An unlettered cleric, maintained the common saying, was like a knight incapable of fighting. By contrast the term *laicus* or layman, whether applied to a peasant or nobleman, usually denoted illiteracy. Although townsmen were also considered as part of the laity, the disability of illiteracy, fostered by rural conditions, was not appropriate for them. The successful operation of commerce required the ability to read, write, and compute, training which the towns as centers of trade were obligated to furnish. It is doubtful whether from Classical times the lay municipal schools of the Mediterranean cities ever completely disappeared during the early Middle Ages, but by the thirteenth century it is certain that many of the Italian communes were providing education for the laity. In these communal schools lay teachers taught reading, writing, the elements of grammar, foreign languages, arithmetic, the operation of the abacus, rhetoric, and perhaps some elements of law—in short, those subjects useful to commerce. Furthermore, within the Mediterranean cities appeared the profession of the notary, who attended to the legal side of business by transcribing documents, keeping records and certifying contracts. The notaries' place in Bologna in the late thirteenth century is attested by their palace in the center of town. By that time a special school and curriculum had emerged to teach notarial science, for which Bologna was renowned. The result of these communal and notarial schools was to create a small but increasingly influential class of literate laity, which would have been an anomaly in the earlier period. The movement began in Italy, but by the thirteenth century all of western Europe was feeling its effects.

Finally, the expanding urban populations presented new problems to the church. In ecclesiastical terminology those clergy whose primary care was the spiritual needs of the laity were designated as the secular clergy, that is, the clergy who were in the world (*saeculum*). They were distinguished from the monks or the regular clergy, who lived in isolation from the world according to a rule (*regula*) in an effort to seek spiritual perfection. In the early Middle Ages, the secular clergy were organized in territories known as parishes, each with a priest to minister to the inhabitants. These parishes were originally distributed according to the sparse population of a predominantly rural society. With the revival of town life in the eleventh century, this pattern of parish organization was unsuited for the densely settled cities. In response to these new conditions the old parishes were divided and redivided, and new churches proliferated within the towns. On the tiny Ile-de-la-Cité of Paris, for example, fourteen parishes were created in the twelfth century. Another solution to the mounting urban populations was to create collegiate churches which were composed of chapters of clergy known as canons who served populous parishes better than a single parish priest. From early times the bishops' cathedrals contained such chapters, but by the eleventh century other urban churches, such as Sainte-Geneviève and Saint-Victor at Paris, adopted the collegiate form. The multiplication of urban parishes and the appearance of collegiate churches called for the recruitment of more secular clergy. We shall see that this expanding secular clergy drawn to the cities was to assume the leadership in the schools of the twelfth century, particularly in northern France.

Even this increase of the secular clergy was not sufficient to keep pace with the population. By the end of the twelfth century popular heresies sprouted in towns, which suggested that the urban masses were increasingly unchurched. Since new means were required to preach to the city multitudes, a further attempt was made in the early thirteenth century with a new kind of clergy, the Dominican and Franciscan friars. Although Saint Dominic and Saint Francis, the illustrious founders of these two orders, differed in their ideals and personalities, it was Dominic and his followers who eventually set the pattern for the movement as a whole. The friars were considered part of the regular clergy insofar as they lived according to a rule and adopted the traditional vows, particularly that of poverty, but they departed from former monastic ideals by refusing to be cloistered and to remain sheltered from the world. On the contrary, they insisted on freedom of movement to follow and minister to the people wherever they could be found, and their emphasis on personal poverty freed them from church revenues, which entwined the secular clergy in local interests. Hence we have the characteristic picture of the friars, dressed in rags, following the masses and begging their daily bread. Widespread throughout western Christendom the friars owed final allegiance only to the pope and thus they became the agents of papal policies through the West.

The compelling zeal of the Dominicans and Franciscans was to imitate Christ by preaching the Gospel to the multitudes and by exemplifying their message through a pious life of poverty. But preaching required learning and education. As the Dominicans often expressed it: the bow is stretched in learning but the arrow is released in preaching. Immediately after their order was officially sanctioned by the Papacy, the Dominicans headed directly for the centers of learning, founding, for example, the convents of San Domenico at Bologna and Saint-Jacques at Paris. The Franciscans followed somewhat later at San Francesco in Bologna and the Cordeliers in Paris. As the thirteenth century progressed, the friars became an increasingly learned clergy, so that some critics eventually accused them of forgetting their primary purpose in their quest for knowledge. Identified with the university movement at an early stage, they were soon rivaling the secular clergy of northern France for leadership in education. At Paris this competition deteriorated into bitter conflict, but by mid-century it was clear that the greatest intellects of the times, at least in theology and philosophy, were to be found among the Dominicans and the Franciscans.

The Monastic Preparation

Schools suffer first and most severely when law, order and stability break down in society. With the collapse of urban institutions in the late Roman Empire came the general dissolution of the ancient public and municipal system of education. While some schools survived in the lands bordering the Mediterranean, elsewhere in Gaul and northern Europe the Classical educational institutions disappeared. During the chaotic epoch of the early Middle Ages the monks assumed the tasks of learning. Actually the monastery was admirably suited for the preservation of culture in an unsettled age. Governed exclusively by its abbot, it was independent of the political order. Placed in the countryside and enjoying vast landed resources, it was economically self-sufficient. By effectively isolating itself from the confusion of the times the community of monks spun a chrysalis which shielded the tender body of learning during the hard winter of the early Middle Ages. Historians frequently designate the sixth through the eleventh centuries as the monastic centuries of education.

The monk's primary goal was not, of course, to instruct others or to preserve culture, but to serve God by prayer, worship, and spiritual perfection. The Benedictine rule, which established the pattern for western monasticism in the sixth century, nonetheless prescribed fixed hours of the day for sacred reading (*lectio divina*). By reading the Bible, the Church Fathers, and other holy works, the monk found spiritual food to sustain his meditations. The institution of *lectio divina*, therefore, required that each monastery possess a library and that each monk be literate. After the ancient schools no longer functioned, the monasteries found it necessary to provide schools for their own community, especially when it became increasingly customary for parents to devote children as oblates to the monastic vocation.

SCHOOLS AND UNIVERSITIES

3

Since the monastery school frequently provided the only instruction in its region, monks came under added pressure to permit neighboring children into their classrooms. The presence of outsiders, who had no commitment to monastic ideals, was naturally a source of distraction to the oblates and of worldly intrusion into the secluded cloister. One solution to this problem was to divide instruction between an internal school for the oblates and an external school, attached to the monastery, but on the outside, for all others. Although such a solution could be afforded by the more wealthy establishments, monks nonetheless remained ambivalent about the propriety of their educational tasks. The love of God and the desire for learning were obviously related, but they could also create conflicts. While Cassiodorus had shown the way in the sixth century for founding a school at his monastery at Vivarium and by composing an educational manual for monks, the great heroes of the monastic movement, Benedict of Nursia and Pope Gregory the Great, were more equivocal. Both had undertaken studies and later renounced them for a higher calling. Because of these examples and practical difficulties, monks retained troubled consciences about their roles as educators.

Through the long centuries of the early Middle Ages the monks placed their imprint on the character of learning. The monastery sheltered an elite community which not only strove for spiritual perfection apart from a grossly imperfect world, but which was also chosen from the highest ranks of society. From the beginning, monks were normally drawn from the free classes, and as gradations of nobility appeared in medieval society, the cloister relied on these well-born families for members. Both spiritually and socially the monk was the aristocrat of the clergy. As successor to the angels on earth he spared no expense or effort to render beautiful his devotion to God. Whenever he drafted letters, composed sermons, or recorded his meditations, he was always anxious that they be well written. To perfect the literary quality of his works he collected and read the writings of Classical Antiquity. Pagan Virgil, Cicero or even Ovid contributed their eloquence to the glory of God. When the monk copied books for his library, he lavished on them expensive parchment, colored inks, and gold leaf as well as painstaking care to transcribe, correct and illuminate them. The production of a book was like prayer and fasting, an authentic service to God. The great beauty of monastic manuscripts are testimony to the monks' patience and devotion. Unconcerned by the passage of time or the conflicts of the world, secure in his rural seclusion, the monk cultivated his learning in isolation. To broaden his horizons he sent letters in the place of travel. His habitat was best depicted by Anthony of the Desert, the fourth-century father of Christian monasticism: "Sit in thy cell and thy cell will teach thee all things. The monk out of his cell is like a fish out of water."

Despite this ideal the chaotic conditions of early medieval society made intruding demands on monastic isolation. Not only were monks asked to maintain schools, but to provide hospitals for the sick, furnish relief for the poor, bury the dead, and perform the sacraments for the laity. When the secular clergy, however, regained strength because of the demographic increase and urban revival of the eleventh century, they began to contest the monk's right to preach and perform the sacraments for the laity. In particular, they sought to regain their former jurisdiction over marriages, burials and tithes, which brought in income. As part of this movement to restrict the external ministry of the monks, the secular clergy also disputed the monastic right to conduct schools. "If you are a monk," wrote one twelfth-century urban canon, "what are you doing in the midst of the crowds? I wish to instruct others, you say. This is not your office; your office is to weep. In fleeing the world, you instruct yourself more than in seeking the world." Increasingly, the monk was encouraged to return to the seclusion of his cloister. In 1163, Pope Alexander III formally forbade monks from leaving their monasteries to study law and medicine, two subjects which involved them directly in worldly affairs. Medicine had the added disadvantage of bringing monks into close contact with women which might compromise their vows of chastity.

The monastic reaction to this challenge from the secular clergy was to withdraw from and even turn against the former educational tasks. For example, the abbey of Cluny, the foremost house of its day, abandoned its external schools in the twelfth century. Guibert of Nogent, who has provided one of the rare autobiographical accounts of the late eleventh century, tells us that when he entered the monastery of Saint-Germer-de-Fly, he was obliged to discontinue his studies, despite the presence of his former teacher, who was also a member of the community. To pursue his scholarly interests he was obliged to read at night, shielded by his covers, because of the displeasure of his fellow monks. This new reaction against the school was best embodied in the Cistercian order, which was the most popular and vigorous monastic reform movement in the twelfth century. The Cistercians fled the world by isolating themselves in wild and uninhabited regions. Emphasizing the duty of manual labor over other forms of service, they excluded the external schools from their constitution and minimized the internal schools by admitting candidates only at an age when the elements of education would have been acquired. To justify their reform, they denounced the new schools of the secular clergy in the towns. The outstanding leader of the Cistercians, and indeed the dominating figure of the first half of the twelfth century, was Bernard, Abbot of Clairvaux (d. 1153). One of his spectacular feats was to conduct an evangelistic mission at Paris in an effort to convert students to holy living and in particular to enlist recruits for the Cistercian order. "Flee this Babylon," he pleaded with his audience, "and save your souls. Fly to the monasteries of the wilderness where solitary rocks and forests teach more piety than mortal masters." In phrases which inspired subsequent monastic authors, he contrasted the harmony, serenity and certitude of the cloister school where Christ was the sole master with the contention, disputation, and doubt of the urban school where fallible masters held their lessons. Undoubtedly Bernard's reaction represented a return to the old hesitations of Benedict and Gregory towards education, but it also voiced a new hostility towards the growing towns. Rupert, the contemporary Abbot of Deutz, thumbed the pages of the Bible for examples of God's displeasure with cities. Cain, the first murderer, was the founder of urban life, and Jericho was dismantled by the people of God. Babel, Babylon, Assur, and Ninevah were all objects of divine wrath, and modern cities represented the resurrection of Sodom and Gomorrah.

The last great intellect of the monastic centuries of education was Anselm, the saintly Abbot of Bec in Normandy who later reluctantly became the Archbishop of Canterbury (d. 1109). Monk, prior, and abbot of this small monastery for thirty years at the turn of the eleventh century, Anselm worked and meditated in comparative isolation, surrounded only by a handful of disciples. Whether he wrote letters of friendship, composed devotional prayers, or constructed philosophic arguments to prove the existence of God, he added a touch of creative originality nourished by the security of the cloister. A half-century later Bernard of Clairvaux repudiated the intellectual role of Anselm of Bec. A man of equal genius, Bernard nonetheless exemplified the abandonment of education by the monks of the twelfth century. After Anselm, the next outstanding figure in scholastic thought was Peter Abelard, but between them an educational revolution had taken place. Learning passed from the rural monastery to the urban school.

The Age of Individualism

The academic careers of Peter Abelard and his student John of Salisbury give us the flavor of the new twelfth-century scene. The son of a Breton knight, Abelard (d. 1142) passionately studied philosophy at Loches and Paris, and theology at Laon. Once a teaching master himself, he transported his school restlessly to Notre-Dame and Sainte-Geneviève in Paris, Melun and Corbeil in the Ile-de-France, and other scattered localities in Champagne. Partly pursued by academic enemies, partly attacking other professors, but always surrounded by a retinue of admiring students,

Abelard became a baron of the schools seeking academic glory on tourney. His younger English contemporary, John of Salisbury (d. 1180), likewise has left a vivid account of his student career during which he attended the lectures at Paris of at least eight different masters on a great variety of subjects for some twelve years. These two scholars stood at the frontier of a new era of education enlivened by enthusiasm, informality, improvisation and flux. The new heroes were the individual teachers like Abelard, who by brilliance of mind and personality drew crowds of admirers to his lessons. Rejecting the seclusion and immobility of the monks, the new masters and students imitated the itinerant habits of the merchant in an effort to seek and exchange the wares of knowledge.

The proliferation of schools clearly benefited from the urban revival in western Europe. Masters were invariably attracted to populous centers in their search for larger audiences. Since, as we shall see, most teachers and students were members of the secular clergy at least in northern Europe, schools were often held in cathedral cloisters or other urban churches. Although some cathedral schools had been established in the early Middle Ages, the Papacy made a new attempt to encourage them in the twelfth century. At the Lateran Council of 1179 Pope Alexander III asked each cathedral chapter to support a teacher who would teach the elements of grammar freely to poor students. By the succeeding Lateran Council of 1215 Pope Innocent III complained that the former decree was not widely effective, but he renewed it and requested metropolitan chapters to provide an additional master in theology. Although these papal decrees expressed ideals more than realities, they indicated the importance of the cathedral school. Like most urban schools in the twelfth century, such schools were centered on the single master. At the end of the century Stephen Langton, a theologian at Paris, provides a glimpse of this situation. Commenting on the Gospel account of Christ calling his disciples, Langton compared it to students entering the schools. First they seek the name of a master whose class they wish to attend and hear his lessons a time or two. If they are pleased, they enter his group, and if they are successful, they are assigned a place in the school and become full disciples.

Since the individual master constituted the school, each school became specialized in the master's interests. Among the scores of urban schools which dotted the map of western Europe, each city became known for an academic specialty. Early in the twelfth century, Chartres retained a reputation for the liberal arts, which Orléans later shared, but preeminence in this subject was undoubtedly enjoyed by Paris throughout the Middle Ages. Paris was also the outstanding center for theology, but early in the twelfth century she was rivaled by Reims and Laon. The cathedral school at Toledo was known for its translations of Greek and Arabic scientific works. Medicine flourished in the Mediterranean cities of Salerno and Montpellier, and while law was taught at Paris, Orléans, and Montpellier, it was the chief subject of Bologna. This specialization of studies was observed by a preacher in the early thirteenth century who remarked somewhat caustically: "In Paris the scholars seek the arts, in Orléans the Classical authors, in Bologna law codices, in Salerno gallipots, in Toledo demons—but nowhere good manners."

The Emergence of Universities

By the end of the twelfth century some semblance of order emerged within the turbulent crowds of scholars. Certain pressing conditions induced both students and masters to set about organizing themselves in a more effective manner. Stimulated by the economic expansion, the numbers of scholars multiplied at an accelerating rate, so that by the thirteenth century the academic population in the chief university towns comprised probably roughly ten per cent of the total inhabitants. With increasing numbers came the need for regulation. The reputation of the schools of Bologna and Paris, moreover, began to overshadow the rest. To these centers masters and students were drawn from all over western Europe. In thirteenth-century Paris, for example, the outstanding professors came from Italy, England, and Germany; few Frenchmen of any importance were to be found among the faculty by mid-century. Although scholars came from countries speaking different tongues, Latin was the common language of instruction. If ever there was a universal republic of letters, it existed in the medieval schools. To the local townsmen, however, these scholars were foreigners, without legal rights and at the mercy of the landlords, shopkeepers, and even the police. For their mutual protection the masters and students had to organize. Since the example closest at hand for such a purpose in the medieval city was the guild, the scholars could consider themselves engaged in a trade or craft and organize for their mutual benefit.

The application of the guild system to education resulted in the universities of the thirteenth century. Terminology clearly points to the origins. A university was simply a *universitas* or a sworn society of students or masters bound together for their mutual protection. In the medieval sense a university was never a place but a group of men. Eventually they were headed by a rector, whose title was also borrowed from the guilds. One of the characteristic preoccupations of these corporations was the regulation of admission to membership, to which end the universities generally were divided into units called nations, which also helped to satisfy the needs of an international body of scholars. The need for protecting common rights made these societies of students or masters tough and effective in urban politics. Among their strengths was poverty in material possessions. They were poor corporations, owning no immoveable property in lands or buildings which could be easily confiscated by the town authorities. The scholars' chief weapon, therefore, was the boycott or strike. When grievances were not rectified, the university, not bound by material ties, could cease its lectures and withdraw to another city. The prospect of a significant element of the population leaving town was accompanied by such economic consequences that the municipal authorities were generally responsive to the demands of the scholars. The freedom to strike was as precious to the university as it is to labor unions today.

Bologna

Corporate organization of scholars first appeared at the turn of the twelfth and thirteenth centuries in Bologna and Paris, the two foremost universities of the Middle Ages, whose example was later followed by other European universities. But these two set different patterns: Bologna was a student university, while Paris belonged to the masters.

By the end of the twelfth century Bologna's preeminence in the study of law was widely recognized. The university originated among the students of law, many of whom were both foreigners and laymen and therefore vitally in need of mutual protection. For the most part, the professors of law were either Bolognese citizens or clerics who were immune to this problem. Gradually and spontaneously the corporations of students emerged with elected councillors and rectors at their head. Alarmed at the potential strength of these groups, the commune of Bologna outlawed their organization by claiming that the students were not an independent trade but merely the pupils of the law professors. The students retaliated with a series of strikes and migrations to nearby Padua. Finally under pressure from the Papacy on behalf of the students and from the threatening loss of business, the commune generally conceded the essentials of guild organization by 1245, and in particular it allowed the right of students to bind themselves by oaths and to elect rectors. This crucial step once taken, the commune showered all kinds of privileges and benefits upon the university to compete with other towns for more students. For the Bolognese citizens, university business was good business.

The university structure of Bologna became fully apparent by the second half of the thirteenth century. The law students were organized in two universities, one for Italians, the other for those from beyond the Alps, or the Ultramontanes. Each of these universities was further divided into nations, the Ultramontanes, for example, into some fourteen separate groups. Eventually the students of arts and medicine formed their respective universities, which cooperated with the more numerous law students on essential matters. It is clear that the professors of law also organized their own guilds by the beginning of the century, but their later appearance and their less urgent needs allowed them to slip under the students' jurisdiction. The chief reason for student domination over teachers was economic. Since many professors were laymen and did not hold ecclesiastical benefices, they were dependent on fees for their instruction. Even at the end of the century when salaried municipal chairs for professors were created, at Bologna they were assigned by student vote. The students, therefore, closely regulated the master's life. He was required to seek a leave of absence from the student rector if he wished to cease lecturing even for a day. If he wished to leave town, he had to post bond. For each day that he failed to attract an audience of less than five, he was treated as absent and fined. His punctuality was strictly enforced, and his lectures had to keep pace with prescribed dates on a syllabus. The only exclusive right possessed by the professor over the students at Bologna, as we shall see, was the admission of candidates to degrees.

Paris

In contrast to Bologna, the universities forming at Paris at about the same time were composed of masters. The most striking difference, which might help to explain this divergence, was that masters and students at Paris were clerics for the most part. From the beginning, students as well as masters possessed essential rights of protection derived from their ecclesiastical status. Regular incomes from church benefices, more prevalent among teachers, were not unknown even among students. Although in certain cases masters regularly collected fees from their students, yet a number of the more renowned enjoyed the economic independence of church livings. Furthermore, at Paris the professors were more international in origin than those of Bologna, and therefore needed greater protection as strangers. Both the students and teachers of arts outnumbered by far the other disciplines. Since these arts students were younger than their Bolognese contemporaries in law, and their masters were more numerous, the university of Paris originated as societies of masters. Students obtained their rights only through association with their professors.

Corporations of masters at Paris went back to the end of the twelfth century, but the definition of their rights and organization emerged in the following century through disputes with the authorities. The chief opponent, as will be seen, was the Chancellor of Notre-Dame, who issued teaching licenses, but conflicts also occurred with the civil powers. Almost invariably clashes arose over the treatment of scholars involved in town and gown riots which periodically enlivened the Paris scene. The first recorded disturbance occurred in 1200 when King Philip Augustus hastily confirmed the scholars' ecclesiastical privileges for fear that the masters would leave town. The *cause célèbre*, however, took place in the pre-Lenten season of 1229 as a result of a general mêlée between students and townsmen in the Faubourg Saint-Marcel where several scholars were killed by the police. Without considering the question of which party was in the wrong, the masters demanded the severe punishment of the officials who had caused the death of the clerics. When the queen mother, who was then governing France in behalf of the young Louis IX, supported the royal police, the masters suspended lectures and later left Paris. This cessation and dispersion of the university lasted until 1231, when finally the bourgeoisie and the Papacy persuaded the royal government to accede to the masters' demands. At that time Pope Gregory IX published a bull which clearly defined the university's essential rights. Not only were the masters recognized as a corporation with full authority to make and enforce statutes, but they were also guaranteed the right of boycott. Since the popes generally supported the university in its struggle for recognition throughout the thirteenth century, the university of Paris became the favorite daughter of the Papacy.

At the middle of the century the university corporation faced a final threat to its privileges. In 1253 another pre-Lenten riot erupted, another scholar was killed, and lectures again ceased. This time the Dominican and Franciscan professors refused to comply with the strike. In accordance with their right to discipline membership, the secular masters expelled the friars from the university because the friars were enjoying the privileges of the society without submitting to its authority. Since the friars were also the chief rivals to the leadership of the secular clergy in learning, the issues went deeper. After a tumultuous period in which the Papacy alternated its support between the friars and the secular masters, the university eventually gained the upper hand and friars quietly submitted on this issue. It is interesting to note that it was in the heat of this controversy that the two outstanding scholars of the Franciscan and Dominican orders, Bonaventure and Thomas Aquinas, were admitted into the society of masters at Paris.

The university consisted of four faculties composed of professors who were actively teaching at Paris. Three higher faculties of theology, canon law and medicine comprised a handful of masters, each headed by a dean. The lower faculty of liberal arts numbered hundreds of teachers and was divided into four nations, each presided over by a proctor. Leadership for all the faculties was provided by the rector. Originally the elected head of the masters of arts, the rector through the command of numbers and responsibility for finances eventually represented the whole university. As a poor corporation, the university borrowed churches for its faculty meetings, most often the little church of Saint-Julien-le-Pauvre, which stands today on the Left Bank opposite Notre-Dame, or the Dominican convent on the rue Saint-Jacques. Its sessions could be almost as disorderly as student behavior in streets of the Latin Quarter.

Most of the universities which were founded in the thirteenth century imitated Paris and Bologna in one way or another. The English universities of Oxford and Cambridge, which excelled in arts and theology, followed Paris and its corporation of masters. Others in Italy, such as Padua, and those specializing in law, such as Orléans in France, followed the student organization of Bologna. Their imitation was the sincerest form of flattery. One should also remember that at this time no universities appeared in Germany; here we have mute testimony to the confusion within the German lands of the Empire. In the twelfth and thirteenth centuries German students usually sought learning in Italy and France. Not until the late Middle Ages did they establish universities of their own.

Academic Degrees

Although the Gospels warned the Christian against seeking the title of master through vainglory, in theory every medieval student set it as the goal of his academic career. Since a master or a doctor (there was still no distinction in the thirteenth century between the titles) was essentially one who had the authority to teach, academic degrees and the profession of teaching were identical. Two separate sets of conditions regulated the admission to degrees. In northern Europe where education was largely the secular clergy's responsibility, the right or license to teach (*licentia docendi*) was controlled by ecclesiastical authority. Every cathedral, collegiate or parish church had the authority to license teachers within its parochial jurisdiction. By the twelfth century this regulation was generally localized, which reflected the profusion and diversity of schools of that period. The ecclesiastical officer responsible for licensing teachers was the *écolâtre* (the chief master of the church schools), the Chancellor, or some other dignitary of the chapter. At Paris, for example, the right to teach was conferred by the Chancellor of Notre-Dame on the Ile-de-la-Cité or by the Abbot of Sainte-Geneviève on the Left Bank. Much of Abelard's misfortune resulted from his difficulties in obtaining this license at Paris and Laon. When the Papacy began to take special interest in educational matters in the twelfth century, it attempted both to regulate and to encourage these licenses. Pope Alexander III confirmed to each *écolâtre* or equivalent church official the right to bestow the *licentia docendi,* but forbade him from discouraging candidates by exacting fees. When in the early thirteenth century Pope Honorius III decreed that Bolognese degrees should be granted with the concurrence of the Archdeacon of Bologna, he was extending to the south a system of ecclesiastical regulation similar to that of Paris.

Although such regulation was known in southern Europe, a rival system for conferring degrees held sway, particularly at Bologna. The societies of law professors retained one essential privilege of admitting to their ranks qualified candidates. This bestowal of the master's degree was fundamentally the guild's right of controlling membership. Even at a later date the Archdeacon of Bologna, a lawyer himself, dared not interfere with this essential authority. The southern system, as it may be called, appeared in Paris early in the thirteenth century with the development of masters' corporations, and because of its late arrival, it clashed with the more established system of ecclesiastical regulation. The societies of masters disputed long and bitterly with the Chancellor of Notre-Dame, whose position was compromised by the alternative authority of the Abbot of Sainte-Geneviève. Eventually through the intervention of the Papacy in support of the university, a solution was reached by which the Chancellor would not refuse to license any candidate proposed by the corporation of masters. But the initial conflict between the Chancellor and the university over the degree remained potentially in the background. For example, during the crisis between the friars and the secular masters, the Chancellor granted licenses to Bonaventure and Thomas Aquinas, but the masters nonetheless refused to admit them to their society. Not until the Papacy applied special pressure were these distinguished scholars allowed into university membership. In the thirteenth century Bologna's and Paris' prestige was so great that their degrees were tacitly accepted throughout western Christendom. To rival this privilege, popes and emperors later bestowed the right of teaching everywhere (*ius ubique docendi*) to lesser institutions.

The kinship between the universities and the guilds is best illustrated by the stages and degrees of an academic career. Full membership in the society was accorded to the master, a title shared with the guilds. The procedure admitting to this title was called the *inceptio* or the initiation, which involved a series of examinations and ceremonies. Although differing according to subject and place, in general it consisted of examinations on contents of knowledge, the demonstration of ability to lecture and dispute, the ceremonial investing of the profession's symbols, and a banquet at the candidate's expense. In essence the *inceptio* embodied the guild principle of entrance into the society upon the successful performance of professional skills. At the intermediate stage towards the master's status was the bachelor. As the journeyman of the professors who was working at the skill, but had not yet acquired full maturity and independence, the bachelor lectured and disputed with certain limitations. At the bottom of the scale were the ordinary students who corresponded to the apprentices of the guilds. The length of time required to obtain a degree varied greatly. In the thirteenth century, for example, a master of arts of Paris took four to five years, a master of theology required about twelve years beyond the arts training. At Bologna canon law might take six years or Roman law eight years beyond the arts, and degrees tended to take longer in the later Middle Ages.

Student Behavior

As a class, scholars succeeded by the thirteenth century in accumulating an impressive list of specific privileges which protected the essential conditions of academic living. Rents on their housing were controlled. Prices and accuracy of their manuscript books were inspected. Their chattels (meaning often their books) were immune from confiscation for the non-payment of rent. Incompatible occupations which produced disturbing noises or obnoxious smells were banned from their sections of town. They were frequently exempt from taxes, levies, tolls, and military service required from the bourgeoisie at home, and were often free from tolls and customs while traveling to and from the schools. Most important, scholars enjoyed a legal status which conferred fundamental benefits on them as a group. In northern Europe both masters and students were clerics, which afforded them the full rights of the church. Even within the clergy they sometimes occupied a privileged place. Students were exempt from local ecclesiastical authorities and subject only to the jurisdiction of their masters. At Paris, moreover, masters and students were under the special protection of the pope, so that they could not be excommunicated *en masse* by the local bishop without permission of the Papacy. In the Mediterranean lands their position was somewhat different. While a number of Italian scholars were clerics, the greater part retained their lay status. The perseverance of urban lay schools, the greater proportion of literate laity, and the practical nature of law and medicine which characterized Italian learning probably account for the difference, but even in Italy masters and students retained privileges not unlike those of the more clerical north. In the *Authentica habita* of 1158 the German Emperor Frederick Barbarossa guaranteed to scholars studying in northern Italy safe conduct in Imperial lands, exemption from reprisals, and most important, the right to decline the legal jurisdiction of the towns for that of the masters or the bishops. The scholar, both clerical and lay, enjoyed a privileged position in medieval society equal to if not greater than the nobility, townsman, or even the clergy.

In northern Europe masters and students almost always claimed full clerical status. This did not imply that they were necessarily in the major orders of priest, deacon or subdeacon or even in the minor orders such as psalmists, readers or acolytes, but merely under the jurisdiction and protection of the church. Clerical status was outwardly designated by the tonsure, the shaving of the crown of the head by the bishop during the mass. Restrictions and obligations resulting from this act were surprisingly slight. Celibacy was required only from priests, deacons, and by the early thirteenth century, subdeacons. Clerics in minor orders and without orders were permitted to marry provided they resign their ecclesiastical benefice. Marriage was therefore possible to masters and students and chiefly a hindrance to those holding benefices and desiring advancement in the church. The relationship between clerical celibacy and scholarship was dramatically illustrated by the personal misfortunes of Peter Abelard. As Abelard himself recounts the story, at the height of his academic career he recklessly fell in love with Héloise, the young niece of canon Fulbert in whose house he was lodging. The lovers' history ran its accustomed course: seduction, an affair, discovery, and pregnancy. Abelard's attempt to pacify the uncle with a secret marriage only enraged him, and when Fulbert became suspicious of treachery, he had the hapless scholar cruelly mutilated. Throughout the affair and the subsequent exchange of letters, Héloise resisted marriage with idealistic consistency. An authentic exponent of pure love, she believed that marriage and a family were incompatible with the scholarly vocation of her lover. Therefore, she was content to remain no more than his faithful mistress. With an uncharacteristic lack of perception, Abelard yearned for a brilliant church career and yet was unable to consent to the gross immorality proposed by Héloise. His unsatisfactory compromise of a secret marriage led to his personal tragedy. Throughout the affair, however, there was never question that Abelard's clerical status or his teaching career would have been endangered by marriage. A public marriage would only have deprived him of his benefice and the chance of future church promotion.

Clerical status conferred two important legal protections upon masters and students. The first, which was entitled the *privilegium canonis*, endowed clerics with a sacred status. To lay violent hands on a clergyman was a sacrilege which incurred automatic excommunication of such gravity that it could be only absolved by a penitential visit to the pope. In ecclesiastical law, clerics enjoy personal inviolability. Even in the Middle Ages when men were not known for their gentleness, one thought twice before he roughed up someone displaying the tonsure. Perhaps such complete protection might have been more plausible if all clerics were mature, responsible men, but it was less appropriate for schoolboys below the age of puberty. During the twelfth century, therefore, canonists were obliged to devise exceptions to the penalty of the *privilegium canonis*. If a teacher birched his pupils or other clerics under the age of puberty, if anyone acted in playfulness or self defense, or if a lay official exercised his just duties—all these cases of clerical assault were either exempt from excommunication or could be absolved by the local bishop. Despite these qualifications, the *privilegium canonis* remained an important protection for scholars. After the Paris riot of 1200 King Philip Augustus promised the masters and students that he would lend royal support to this clerical privilege. The bourgeoisie took an oath to apprehend and testify against anyone assaulting a cleric, and the *prévôt*, the royal officer in charge at Paris, was responsible for investigating the enforcement of these provisions.

Closely related to the *privilegium canonis* was a second legal protection, the *privilegium fori* which placed clerics under the exclusive jurisdiction of the church courts. Because of the *Authentica habita*, the lay scholar of Italy as well as the clerical scholar of the north had the right to refuse the royal and municipal courts for ecclesiastical jurisdiction over all crimes, even gross felonies such as murder, rape, arson and armed robbery. Since the *privilegium canonis* prevented the church court from administering corporal punishment, the ecclesiastical judge could condemn gross crimes only with sentence of excommunication, penance, and degradation (loss of clerical status). Wherever clerics were in large numbers, their immunity against criminal prosecution posed a serious threat to the public peace.

The problem of criminous clerics, however, was further complicated by a specific dispute between King Henry II of England and Thomas Becket, Archbishop of Canterbury. In an effort to safeguard the rights of the clergy and yet to prosecute clerical crimes more effectively, King Henry proposed an elaborate procedure in the Constitutions of Clarendon of 1164. A criminous cleric was to be apprehended and accused by the royal justice and then turned over to a church court to be tried according to canon law but in the presence of a royal official. If the ecclesiastical judge found the cleric guilty, he was to be degraded of his clerical status and handed over to the royal court for due punishment. Since the degraded cleric no longer benefited from his clerical privileges, he could be punished as a layman. Opposing several features of this procedure, the archbishop objected most strenuously to the handing over of the cleric to the royal judge after degradation. In Becket's view degradation was sufficient punishment for the crime and a corporal penalty from the royal court would amount to double punishment or double jeopardy. Of course, additional crimes could be prosecuted by the royal courts, but in effect every cleric had the right to one crime without corporal punishment. The conflict between the king and archbishop over this point resulted eventually in Becket's martyrdom, and a revulsion of public opinion forced Henry to accept the archbishop's position.

After the Paris riot of 1200, the French King Philip Augustus was likewise obliged to adopt Becket's treatment of criminous clerics. Although the *prévôt* could apprehend an accused cleric, he had to treat him with extreme care and turn him over immediately to the church courts. (If the ecclesiastical judge were inaccessible at night, the cleric would not be jailed with common criminals but kept separate in a student hostel until the church authorities were available.) When the *prévôt* turned over the accused cleric to the church judge, his responsibility ended. At Paris, where young clerical scholars comprised a substantial segment of the population, this procedure was not helpful in resolving the problem of clerical crime. Finally, five years later the king negotiated a more satisfactory compromise with the church. While an ecclesiastical judge was not required to hand over a degraded cleric directly to the royal authorities, neither was he permitted to release him in a church or cemetery where he could claim asylum. Rather, the church court promised to release the convicted and degraded cleric in a place where the royal justices could apprehend and punish him without incurring the anathemas of the *privilegium canonis*. Where Henry II had failed in England, Philip Augustus succeeded in France by establishing a procedure for dealing more effectively with clerical crime.

The outcome of this issue was particularly significant for Paris where masters and students were numerous. Undoubtedly the privileged status of scholars had a marked effect on student behavior. Shielded by his clerical tonsure and subject to a separate and more lenient jurisdiction, the student was a hard person to discipline. The rioting before Lent on the Left Bank occurred all too regularly to be attributed to accidental causes. One can readily sympathize with the good Parisian burghers who complained that the safety of their women and the peace of their houses were continually threatened by marauding student bands. Indeed, King Philip Augustus once marvelled that the aggressive instincts of clerics exceeded even those of knights. While knights fought only in armor, clerics sprang into the fray without helmets to protect their clean-shaven pates. But the king had actually little cause to wonder, because he knew, as well as anyone, that the tonsure, the outward sign of clerical status, was more of a protection than the helmet.

Uninhibited behavior was further accentuated by the lack of maturity among the Paris scholars. One of the common complaints of contemporary observers and moralists was that masters were beginning to teach before they had acquired sufficient knowledge. Pink-cheeked youths were mounting professional chairs to display their fatuous ignorance. This criticism implied that the Chancellor of Notre-Dame and the Abbot of Sainte-Geneviève were not rigorous enough in issuing licenses to teach. "Believe only the bearded master" became the slogan of the critics. In 1215 a papal legate decreed that a master of arts must have achieved his twenty-first year after six years of study and that a master of theology must be at least thirty-five and have studied for eight years.

At no time were the ebullient energies of youth more evident in Paris than during the ecclesiastical festivities at the end of the year. A series of feasts assigned to the younger clergy provided opportunity for their unconventional behavior. On the Feast of Saint Nicholas (December 6) a young cleric was elected boy bishop who was to preside over the other festivals. On the Feast of the Innocents (December 28) the choir boys assisted him in boisterous celebrations. The climax of the year was achieved on the Feast of the Circumcision (January 1) which was assigned to the subdeacons. Known also as the Feast of the Fools, it consisted of processions through town and special services conducted by the young clergy. Since the liturgy concerned the flight into Egypt, clerics impersonated Joseph and Mary and even introduced a live donkey into the church, so that the service was later known as the Office of the Ass. The representations became so realistic that swords were employed and blood shed. This celebration also afforded ample opportunity for outrageous parody of the divine services as well as riotous revelry in which bystanders were often pommelled with inflated bladders. There is little doubt that the students and young masters could have been excluded from the fun. After all, Saint Nicholas was their patron saint.

Animated by youthful exuberance, protected from the local police, at liberty to pursue their studies anywhere, these young scholars often lived at the margin between the urban underworld and decent society. By the twelfth century students who wandered from town to town in search of famous masters formed an *ordo vagorum*, an order of wanderers, in impious parody of the monastic and priestly orders of the day. Their besetting sins were the well-known trilogy of dice, wine and wenches. Supporting themselves as entertainers, jongleurs, and mere vagrants they created a literature of verse to celebrate their pleasures. Known as Goliardic poetry, from the name of Golias, who was the mythical head of this wandering order, their writing ranges from lyrical love poetry to bawdy verse. Undoubtedly much of the debauchery portrayed is adolescent exaggeration, but these medieval students created a tradition of bohemian living which has found its devotees ever since. As this unconventional behavior increased in notoriety, the ecclesiastical authorities could no longer ignore the Goliards. In the mid-thirteenth century a series of French councils anathematized the movement and threatened degradation. Without clerical status the wandering scholar's existence became precarious, and the Goliards finally disappeared.

The Economics of Learning

In the Middle Ages, as in every age, students financed their studies from family resources or from individual ingenuity or industry. Gifts and loans for study became so valuable that students compiled manuals containing model letters for requesting money from fathers, uncles, affluent ecclesiastics, and other potential patrons. Attempting to impress a prospective donor with the writer's learning, one model letter adapted a famous line from Terence for its particular purpose: "For you must know that without Ceres (bread) and Bacchus (wine) Apollo (learning) shivers in the cold." (This quotation, however, might have been dangerous because if the recipient was familiar with the original verse, he might have been suspicious of the student's seriousness. It referred to Venus rather than Apollo.) If one were not so fortunate to possess affluent benefactors, one could employ his talents as a tutor, preceptor, choir boy or entertainer for pay. But in northern Europe where most students were clerics, they enjoyed a decided advantage over their lay counterparts in the south. Clerical status offered a number of economic benefits to the scholar.

Not the least of these advantages was free housing. Since students belonged to the clergy, early in the twelfth century pupils of the school of Notre-Dame were lodged in the cloister. As the school increased in fame and its numbers grew, it became increasingly difficult to find room for them. By 1127 no more students from outside the diocese were allowed in the cloister. By the 1160's even the canons of Notre-Dame were forbidden to rent their houses to scholars, such as Fulbert had done for Abelard. With this opportunity restricted, students rented lodgings in private residences, the houses of masters, and hostels on the Ile-de-la-Cité and eventually on the Left Bank. So crowded were conditions on the Cité that one preacher reported that scholars and prostitutes often shared the same dwelling. While the master held his school on the upper floor, the women quarrelled with their pimps and exercised their distracting profession below. This housing shortage in the center of

Paris placed students at the mercy of the well-known rapacity of landlords. In order to protect themselves masters and students were permitted in 1215 to enter into agreements supervising the rents of hostels. Although this policy of university rent control was strengthened throughout the thirteenth century, other measures were necessary to replace the facilities of the cloister of Notre-Dame for the poor student. In 1180 a rich Londoner endowed a room in the Hôtel-Dieu across the square from Notre-Dame for the use of eighteen poor scholars. When this group eventually acquired its own building it became known as the Collège des Dix-huit, the first of numerous colleges at Paris. A college was essentially an ecclesiastical and charitable foundation to supply board and room for needy students. Often they were modelled after the Dominican and Franciscan convents, which could be considered as colleges for the friars. The most famous of the Parisian colleges, the Sorbonne, was designed for sixteen poor students embarked on the long career of a theological degree. The English collegiate system in Oxford and Cambridge faithfully reflects the Parisian colleges. When a significant proportion of students became dependent on college benefits, the university had another means for disciplining behavior. Unruly conduct was threatened with expulsion from college, and as a result, student discipline improved appreciably in the later Middle Ages.

Clerical status also made students eligible for an ecclesiastical benefice, which was a regular income assigned to a church to support a cleric who served the church in a specific function. While occasionally benefices were granted for administrative duties in large churches or even for teaching in the cathedral schools, as we have seen, most of them were designated for priests who served the laity as pastors. A benefice for the "cure of souls," as it was called, naturally implied that its holder would remain in the parish to minister the sacraments to his flock. Eventually, however, certain reasons for leaving his church were considered legitimate, if the pastor provided a substitute vicar. Among these were travel to conduct church's business, pilgrimages, and study in the schools. In the twelfth century the canonists and the Papacy argued that if a priest could improve his ministry through better education, he was justified in absenting himself from his parish for the sake of study. By the end of the thirteenth century Pope Boniface VIII regularized this program by encouraging all priests to spend five years in the schools. While he was studying, the pastor was supported by his benefice. Even with this encouragement, however, there were not sufficient benefices for the thousands of students drawn to the schools and universities of western Europe. Since many had no intention of entering the pastorate, they were only eligible for the very few benefices without "cure of souls." A great number were driven to rely on their benefactors, charitable foundations and personal wits. But as clerics they possessed one final resource, the right to beg, and many a poor student managed to survive through the charity of his neighbors.

Enjoying the same clerical status as students, masters were also eligible to profit from the system of ecclesiastical benefices in northern Europe. In 1179 Pope Alexander III ordered each cathedral chapter to assign a benefice to a master who would teach poor students the elements of the liberal arts free of charge. Recognizing the general failure of the former decree, as we have seen, Pope Innocent III nonetheless attempted to extend it to all collegiate churches as well as to add that each metropolitan chapter should support a theological master. Applied to Paris, this papal program was totally devoid of consequence. Single masters at Notre-Dame, Sainte-Geneviève, and Saint-Victor were ridiculously inadequate in the face of the thousands of art students, and the chapter of Notre-Dame was not even required to supply a theologian because it was not of metropolitan rank. As in the case of the students, the assignment of other benefices presented a more realistic solution. By curious logic, "absence for the sake of study" was allowed to masters as well as students with benefices involving the cure of souls. Moreover, as the popes claimed the right to assign more and more benefices throughout the twelfth and thirteenth centuries, they directly bestowed an increasing number on distinguished teachers. But the rise of prices, we remember, brought inflation in the thirteenth century. Since the incomes of benefices were normally fixed, they became insufficient to support their holders, which encouraged churchmen to seek more than one. Since this practice of pluralism, as it was called, accentuated the former evils of absenteeism, it was usually prohibited in canon law, but an exception was created to alleviate the economic distress of masters. At the Lateran Council of 1215 Pope Innocent III decreed that learned men who should be honored with major church benefices may be excused by the pope from the restrictions against pluralism if sufficient reason deemed it necessary. Despite these papal measures to increase benefices for teachers, the supply was never able to keep abreast of the growing demand for new masters. While the more distinguished members of the higher faculties of theology and canon law at Paris may have enjoyed church livings, the hundreds of masters of arts could never hope for such support, and in Italy where the teaching of Roman law and medicine prevailed, lay teachers were not eligible for benefices. Obviously, some solution beyond the benefice was required to finance the expansion of education.

After Abelard's disgrace, he retired to the wilderness of Champagne, where he continued to teach his students. As he expressed it himself, since he could not work with his hands, he worked with his voice, and his disciples paid him for his lessons.

Here is an early example of the academic fee paid directly by the student to the master. Commonly practiced by the thirteenth century when the universities of Paris and Bologna were in full vigor, the academic fee broadened the economic base of learning. In Bologna the professor appointed a student who bargained with his class for the price of his lessons. Yet in the twelfth century Pope Alexander III had enunciated the gratuity of learning as a principle. No fees could be charged for licenses to teach and benefices should be granted to masters to teach poor scholars without charge. It was therefore with an uneasy conscience that masters accepted the system of fees. Before money could be exacted, two sets of conditions were considered: Did the master possess a benefice and what subject did he teach? If he held a benefice designated for teaching (such as the masters in the cathedral schools), he was not allowed to collect fees. If his benefice was not for the purpose of teaching, his case was more doubtful, but if he held no benefice, he could accept money because of his poverty. If he taught theology with a benefice, he was denied fees, but without a benefice, he could accept gifts from his students for his theological lessons as long as he did not make a prior contract. For the instruction of secular subjects such as the liberal arts and law, the distinctions became more refined, but in general if the master possessed no benefice, he could exact fees with a clear conscience. The great majority of masters of arts at Paris and law professors at Bologna were therefore guaranteed this form of income. In the university the academic fee replaced the benefice as the chief economic foundation of learning. But the fee, it should be remembered, afforded the student a lever against the master, particularly in Italy where the student universities were well organized. In order to attract distinguished teachers, communes like Padua began to create salaried chairs paid by public funds, which offered the professor an escape from student domination. But this form of financing was not adopted in the north, and at Bologna even the salaried chairs fell under student influence because their incumbents were elected annually by the student body.

The New Images of Scholarship

The shift from the benefice to the fee signified an important transformation in the image of the scholar in western Europe. In Classical Antiquity the radical division between slaves and freemen produced corresponding distinctions between the mechanical and the liberal arts. Appropriate for slaves, the mechanical arts included agriculture, crafts, and petty commerce, in which physical work played a predominant role. The labor of the artisan could be hired by contract and paid by wages. By way of contrast the liberal arts included the professions of teaching, medicine, and law, which primarily involved intellectual work and were therefore most suitable for free men. Since the Classical free man was assumed to be a gentleman of independent means, it was inappropriate for him to hire his services or to receive wages; rather, he dispensed his skills as an act of friendship in which remuneration was not directly involved. The highest example of the liberal professions in Antiquity was the philosopher, and Socrates was its ideal. As was widely believed, Socrates freely taught philosophy within the circle of his friends and attacked the Sophists for selling knowledge as common merchandise. Socrates accepted gifts from his disciples only when they were offered as acts of gratitude. Later in ancient Roman law the philosopher was allowed to accept but never to demand fees from his pupils. Of course, the ancient view of the intellectual was blurred by complexities and contradictions, but as exemplified by Socrates, the scholar was a free man who imparted wisdom to his friends without thought of direct recompense.

This ancient ideal was perpetuated by the clergy in the early Middle Ages, particularly the monks who exercised the professions of teaching and medicine. As the elite of the clergy, the monks were the worthy successors to the liberal professions because they were personally free and economically secure in their cloisters. Teaching, for example, was a sacred calling for which wages were inappropriate. The principle that knowledge should be dispensed freely was further echoed by the Papacy in the twelfth century. When Pope Alexander III forbade charging for teaching licenses and instituted cathedral masters to instruct poor students without fees, he repeated an old dictum that knowledge was a gift of God and should not be sold. Even in the thirteenth century the theologian retained this ideal. Heir to the Classical philosopher, the theologian without benefice, we remember, was allowed to accept gifts, but never to demand fees from his students.

When urban life revived in the eleventh century in western Europe, a new exemplar appeared for the intellectual—the townsman who specialized his skills, travelled widely, and sold his wares. As we have seen, not only did masters and students follow the pattern of urban guilds when they organized their universities, but the masters also began to collect fees from their students when the old system of benefices became inadequate. To justify this new form of income the scholar began to identify his profession with the mechanical arts. In the early thirteenth century one theologian, for example, equated the teaching of the liberal subjects of language, geometry, and arithmetic with the mechanical skills of the farmer, artisan, and carpenter. If the artisan could exercise his craft at a wage set by contract, why not also the master of arts? The teaching of rudimentary subjects was equivalent to plowing the fields. Like the farmer, the master's recompense was justified by his labor, because, as the Scriptures teach, the laborer is worthy of his hire. Such arguments indicate a transformation in education. No longer belonging to the holy monk in rural isolation, learning has become the property of the urban master who produced his intellectual goods within the *atelier* of his school and sold them to his students at a price to compensate labor and skill. The artisan replaced the monk as the pattern for the scholar.

This desacralization of learning was most graphically illustrated in the transformation of the book in the twelfth century. As a work of penance and devotion, the monastic book of the early Middle Ages contained expensive parchment, gold leaf, wide margins, painstaking script, and artistic illuminations. Such beautiful masterpieces were obviously much too expensive and rare for the thousands of masters and students who thronged the twelfth-century schools. To supply their needs books were mass produced by publishers, known as *stationarii,* who employed scores of copyists working at a feverish rate. Illuminations were eliminated, margins reduced, parchment cheapened, and abbreviations increased within the script. Even the style of lettering was changed from the Carolingian miniscule, which emphasized the curved line, to the new Gothic script, which employed short, straight strokes, capable of more rapid execution. No longer the product and object of religious devotion, the book was changed into the instrument and tool of the artisan master in his urban school.

As the universities matured in western Europe the masters and students began to evaluate their contributions to medieval society. With justified pride they began to compare themselves favorably with such venerable institutions as the Papacy and the Empire, and this desire for recognition led to certain forms of imitation. The Papacy, of course, possessed a hallowed tradition of divine institution perpetuated by apostolic succession from Christ to the most recent pope. The Empire likewise claimed a tradition of *translatio imperii* or the transmission of imperial dignity from the Rome of the Caesars through the Carolingians to the present German rulers of the Holy Roman Empire. Prompted by this imperial tradition, the scholars began to formulate their own legend of *translatio studii.* By the thirteenth century the legend had assumed different forms, but most focused attention on France and the university of Paris. One version envisaged learning originating with the Hebrews, then passing to Egypt, to Athens, to Rome and finally residing at Paris. Another version centered around Saint Denis, whose name and relics were cherished by the royal abbey to the north of Paris. Saint Denis, the patron saint of France, was depicted as Denis or Dionysius, the famed Greek philosopher of ancient times, who was converted to the faith by the Apostle Paul, and who brought both the Gospel and learning to France. The university of Paris, then, was the new Athens, the successor to ancient wisdom. By the end of the thirteenth century Frenchmen were boasting: Italy has the Papacy, Germany has the Empire, but France has the university.

Lectures and Disputations

In his eloquent defense of the liberal arts entitled *The Metalogicon*, John of Salisbury declared:

Our own generation enjoys the legacy bequeathed to it by that which preceded it. We frequently know more, not because we have moved ahead by our own natural ability, but because we are supported by the mental strength of others, and possess riches that we have inherited from our forefathers. Bernard of Chartres used to compare us to puny dwarfs perched on the shoulders of giants. He pointed out that we see more and farther than our predecessors, not because we have keener vision or greater height, but because we are lifted up and borne aloft on their gigantic stature.[1]

Adopted from a well-known phrase of the ancient grammarian Priscian, Bernard's metaphor of dwarfs seated on the shoulders of giants was commonplace in the twelfth century and articulated an underlying medieval respect for past achievement. If present knowledge is built on past wisdom, then all learning must begin with ancient authority. We shall see that each discipline had its authoritative texts: Aristotle for logic, Justinian for Roman law, and the Bible for theology. As a technical term, authority was derived from the Latin word *auctor*, which designated the plaintiff in a law case. From this legal connotation it was clear that authorities could make accusations or begin the discussion, but they did not necessarily determine the conclusions. "Authorities have noses of wax; they can be deflected in different directions" was a popular aphorism in the twelfth century. In other words, although authorities present the initial basis for discussion, they can be interpreted to mean different things. This characteristic role of authoritative texts was influential in shaping the course of medieval education.

[1] John of Salisbury, *The Metalogicon*, trans. D. D. McGarry (Berkeley and Los Angeles, 1955), p. 167.

SECULAR STUDIES: ARTS, MEDICINE, AND LAW

We remember that a candidate was admitted to the master's degree upon the successful demonstration of teaching skills. At the end of the twelfth century, Peter the Chanter, a theologian at Paris, depicted these activities as "reading, disputation, and preaching . . . for reading is, as it were, the foundation or basement for what follows. . . . Disputation is the wall or edifice of study. . . . and preaching, which is supported by the former, is the roof." While the last skill was peculiar to the theologians, the first two, reading and disputation, were the common teaching methods of all disciplines.

Since all learning began with past authority, it was essential to read and master the authoritative text. In a technical sense reading (*lectio*) meant both reading and explaining an authority publicly before a class of pupils. This medieval practice was the forerunner of the modern procedure of lecturing. Generally such lectures were distinguished by the time of day. "Ordinary" lectures conducted by fully qualified professors on the basic texts of the discipline were held in the morning. As the most important sessions they were distinguished from the "extraordinary" or cursory lectures delivered usually in the afternoon, often by bachelors, and more rapidly on less fundamental texts. In effect, extraordinary sessions were designed to supplement the ordinary sessions. Odofredus, a celebrated professor of Roman law at Bologna in the thirteenth century, advertised his lectures in this way:

First, I shall give you summaries of each title before I proceed to the text; secondly, I shall give you as clear and explicit a statement as I can of the purport of each Law (included in the title); thirdly, I shall read the text with a view to correcting it; fourthly, I shall briefly repeat the contents of the Law; fifthly, I shall solve apparent contradictions, adding any general principles of Law (to be extracted from the passage), commonly called "Brocardica," and any distinctions or subtle and useful problems (questiones) *arising out of the Law with their solutions, as far as Divine Providence shall enable me. And if any Law shall seem deserving, by reason of its celebrity or difficulty, of a Repetition, I shall reserve it for an evening Repetition.*[2]

Although instruction was essentially oral in nature, professors often wished to publish their lectures in writing. This was accomplished by officially designating a student, known as a reporter, to take down the substance of the lecture which was then reviewed by the master before it was handed to the copyists for duplication

---

[2] Translated in Hastings Rashdall, *The Universities of Europe in the Middle Ages,* ed. F. M. Powicke and A. B. Emden (Oxford, 1936), I, p. 218. This account was recorded by his student.

and distribution. Designated as *reportationes*, these writings stood between the precise dictation of a stenographer and the informal notes of a student. A vast amount of these writings have survived in the form of commentaries to the basic texts. The works of Aristotle, the compilation of Justinian, and the Bible, to take three characteristic examples, were furnished with thousands of commentaries from the medieval universities. Often they took the form of glosses in which the basic authority occupied the center of the page and the master's comments filled the margins. Prompted by the requirements of mastering authoritative texts, the lecture generated the commentary or gloss as its characteristic mode of expression.

But, as will be seen, authoritative statements have an inveterate habit of disagreeing. The debates thus provoked encouraged various forms of public disputation among the masters of the universities. At times two masters would debate, or one master would defend an announced thesis against all comers. Most professors held a certain number of these exercises, known as *questiones disputatae*, throughout the ordinary sessions of the year. During the Christmas and Easter holidays another type of disputation was conducted, called the *disputatio de quolibet*, in which a master would debate any question with any person. Quodlibet disputations were academic free-for-alls which attracted large audiences because of their spontaneity and capriciousness. Offering ample opportunity for venting scholarly rivalries, they were the academic tournaments in which the medieval professor released his belligerent feelings. By the thirteenth century the procedure for the disputation became standardized and usually lasted two days. On the first day the master, or even his bachelor, received objections to the question and attempted to answer them as best he could. By the end of this session many arguments, objections, and refutations had been collected in great confusion on a particular question. Taking up the question again on the next regular lecture, the master then had opportunity to coordinate the arguments and objections, to propose a solution, and to reduce all to a systematic exposition. This second day was called the master's determination of the question, and in this form the disputation was recorded in writing.

As suggested by Peter the Chanter, the medieval master conceived of himself as constructing an edifice of learning from the elements of reading, disputing and preaching, skills which have since become known as the scholastic method because they were fashioned in the schools. According to its fundamental meaning, the term scholasticism is simply that system of thinking, teaching, and writing produced in the medieval schools. We shall see how these scholastic techniques affected the study of the different disciplines.

The Liberal Arts

In the thirteenth century the university curriculum was divided into four faculties: one lower faculty of liberal arts and three higher faculties of medicine, law, and theology. While other subjects such as engineering and architecture were also offered, they were almost always situated within this framework. Of these studies, three—the arts, medicine, and law—may be considered as secular subjects. Theology, or sacred science, will be kept apart because of its unique importance in the Middle Ages.

Some rudiments of the liberal arts were taught by all local schools whether municipal or ecclesiastical. We have seen how the Papacy attempted to encourage these elementary studies by commanding each cathedral and later each collegiate church to teach grammar freely to those who would learn. But some schools in the twelfth century specialized in the advance study of the liberal arts according to the interests of individual masters. Perpetuating traditions which went back for almost a century, Master Bernard made the school of Chartres celebrated for the liberal arts in the first decades of the twelfth century.[3] Late in the century Orléans was also well known for its interest in Classical literature. Throughout the twelfth century, however, the undisputed center for the advanced study of the liberal arts was Paris. When John of Salisbury arrived in France in the fourth decade of the century in search of liberal learning, a galaxy of renowned masters attracted him to the French capital. There he studied logic under Abelard, Alberic, and Robert of Melun and grammar under William of Conches, and Richard l'Evêque perfected his knowledge of the quadrivium. In John's opinion Paris undoubtedly had the best teachers assembled in any one place. When the university was organized in the thirteenth century, the faculty of arts retained this preeminence.

In Classical civilization the liberal arts formed the basic curriculum appropriate for the training of free men (hence the term, liberal). By late Antiquity they numbered seven and were divided into two groups: the trivium consisting of grammar, logic, and

[3]Beginning in the mid-nineteenth century scholars have maintained that the school of Chartres was a brilliant center for the liberal arts, humanistic studies, Platonism, and natural philosophy. It claimed great teachers such as Bernard of Chartres and William of Conches, distinguished Chancellors such as Thierry of Chartres and Gilbert de la Porrée, and exceptional students such as John of Salisbury. Recently Professor R. W. Southern of Oxford has reexamined the evidence for the school of Chartres and has concluded that support can only be found for Bernard's teaching at the beginning of the century. While Thierry and Gilbert were undoubtedly Chancellors, they actually taught at Paris, as did William of Conches as well. The evidence that John of Salisbury ever studied at Chartres is very slight. The glory of Chartres, Professor Southern argues, is reduced to Bernard, which may explain more easily why the school disappeared in the second half of the century. See R. W. Southern, *Medieval Humanism and other Studies* (Oxford, 1970), pp. 61–85.

rhetoric, and the quadrivium comprising arithmetic, geometry, astronomy, and music (meaning musical theory). This system of elementary education was adopted by the Church Fathers and the monasteries in the early Middle Ages, but not without hesitation, as we shall see. Reflecting his teaching at Paris, Thierry of Chartres composed a guide to the seven liberal arts, appropriately entitled the *Heptateuchon* (the seven), which recommended the prerequisite authorities for each art. For example, the texts for grammar were Donatus, Priscian, and the masterpieces of Latin prose and poetry. Aristotle was the chief authority for logic or dialectics, and Cicero and Quintillian provided basic instruction for rhetoric. Each of the quadrivium had its authorities as well. According to Thierry the division between the quadrivium and the trivium represented the basic separation between the mind and its expression. The quadrivium embodied the contents of knowledge; the trivium its expression with correctness, reason, and eloquence. "It is therefore manifest," Thierry concluded, "that the *Heptateuchon* is the proper and unique instrument of all philosophy. But philosophy is the love of wisdom and wisdom is the complete comprehension of the truth."

Early in the twelfth century, grammar commanded most attention from those who studied the trivium. As John of Salisbury formulated it, "Grammar is the science of speaking and writing correctly—the starting point of all liberal studies. Grammar is the cradle of all philosophy, and in a manner of speaking, the first nurse of the whole study of letters." Derived from the Greek word *gramma* meaning letter, its mastery imparted literacy. By learning its rules one would avoid barbarisms (errors in vocabulary and pronunciation) and solecisms (errors of construction) as well as attain knowledge of figures of speech, metrics, and etymology. The beginner learned Donatus' *Ars minor* by heart (it comprises ten modern pages) before advancing to Donatus' *Ars maior* and Priscian's *Institutio* which provided illustrations from Classical Latin literature. Following this tradition, Bernard of Chartres used to teach grammar in his school by reading Latin authors and explaining them from a grammatical point of view. In effect, early in the twelfth century Bernard was applying the academic technique of reading (*lectio*) to grammatical study. This method was continued by William of Conches, although John of Salisbury complained that it had become outmoded in his day. Bernard's emphasis upon the Latin prose writers and poets gave a literary orientation to grammar, of which John approved. Masters read and produced glosses to Classical literature such as Bernard Sylvester's commentary on the first six books of Virgil's *Aeneid*, which provided an allegorical interpretation of this pagan masterpiece. And in his own writings, John, himself, exhibited first-hand familiarity with a wide range of Classical Latin authors.

Like their monastic predecessors the clerical teachers of France harbored ambivalent feelings about the propriety of studying pagan literature. Although they were assuredly models of style, the Latin Classics were at best expressions of fundamental egoism and at worst frankly lascivious tales, all of which offended Christian sensibilities. The hesitation was as old as the Church Father Jerome in the fourth century. Although he was impressively versed in Classical literature and found it virtually impossible to forget a beautiful line, Jerome once dreamed that he was refused entrance to heaven because of his pagan learning. When Jerome protested that he was a Christian, the supreme judge's awesome reply was: "Liar, you are a Ciceronian, not a Christian." To relieve their scruples and justify Classical literature, the Church Fathers adopted the Scriptural image of the Jews despoiling the Egyptians. Just as the Hebrews had carried out costly raiment and precious jewels on their exodus from Egypt, so Christians could despoil pagan literature of its treasures provided that all was devoted to divine service. Or to change the image, Classical letters became the handmaidens of the mistress theology. Despite this justification, the ambivalence remained. When masters lectured on the Classics they placed greater emphasis on the introductory remarks to the work. Entitled the *accessus*, this preface announced the subject of the work, its author's intentions, its final purpose and place in the scheme of knowledge. During the twelfth century it was lengthened so that the master could take the edge off the offensive barbs of the Classical work and relate its message to Christian truth. In particular, the allegorical interpretation, such as Bernard Sylvester applied to the *Aeneid*, was an appropriate means for rendering Classical letters the servant of theology.

Perched on the shoulders of ancient giants, the medieval master of arts sensed no radical break with the Classical past, yet modern historians have perceived a significant increase of interest in Classical letters in the twelfth century. While the causes of this "renaissance" are under conjecture, the revival of towns appears to have been influential. The specialization of urban life created a demand for particular skills of Antiquity: Roman law for government and commerce, Greek science for medicine, and Aristotelian logic for theology. Similarly, Classical literature produced by an urban civilization provided new inspiration for the medieval townsman. Although the matter has not been fully explored, a civic humanism of the medieval town may have been responsible for the "renaissance" in the twelfth century as it was in the fifteenth century.

If grammar and literature were preeminent among the liberal arts in the first half of the twelfth century, ascendency within the trivium shifted to logic in the second half. Already by the fourth decade of the century, John of Salisbury was alarmed by the rage for dialectics at Paris and objected to those who concentrated attention on this discipline to the exclusion of the other arts. It was Abelard above all who popularized logical studies at Paris. As a young master he first achieved prominence as a skillful dialectician and his prestige attracted students from afar. Throughout Antiquity Aristotle's collection of logical works known as the *Organon* was commonly regarded as authoritative. When Abelard taught dialectics at Paris early in the century only two introductory treatises, the *Categories* and the *Interpretation*, were available in Latin, but during the second quarter of the century the remaining portions of the *Organon* began to circulate. These included the *Prior Analytics*, which dealt with syllogisms and forms common to reasoning, the *Sophistic Refutations*, which listed common fallacies, the *Topics*, which treated probable premises, and the *Posterior Analytics*, which discussed scientific reasoning. Known as the "new logic" to distinguish them from the *Categories* and *Interpretation*, these treatises provided medieval men with the essential techniques of ancient reasoning. So esteemed were the new discoveries that dialectics began to displace and transform the former grammatical and literary interests of the arts masters. While Donatus and Priscian were primarily descriptive and relied on literary usage as their final criterion, the new grammarians attempted to introduce logical considerations. At mid-century, Peter Helias shifted attention from the facts of language to its causes. By the end of the century Alexander of Villedieu assumed the rational character of speech and attempted to reconstruct grammar from logical rules. The ground gained by dialectics is indicated by the first official curriculum for the Paris faculty of arts which appeared in 1215. In place of Latin literature, grammar was limited to the technical treatise of Priscian, and Aristotle's *Organon* with its ancient commentaries formed the bulk of the prescribed texts. The primary duty of the master of arts was to teach dialectics.

This shift from grammar to logic was depicted by the poet Henry of Andeli early in the thirteenth century in an allegorical poem entitled *The Battle of the Seven Arts*. Orléans was chosen to represent the older traditions of grammar now challenged by Paris, which personified the new logic:

Paris and Orléans are at odds.
It is a great loss and a great sorrow
That the two do not agree.
Do you know the reason for the discord?
It is because they differ about learning;
For Logic, who is always wrangling,
Calls the authors authorlings

And the students of Orléans mere grammar-boys.
Each, she says, is well worth four Homers,
For they drink huge bumpers
And are so skillful at versifying
That about a single leaf of a fig-tree
They will compose you fifty verses.
But they retort that verily
They call Dialectic,
In evil spite, a cock-a-doodle-do (quiqueliquique).
As for those of Paris, the clerks of Plato,
They do not think them worth a button.
However, Logic has the students,
Whereas Grammar is reduced in numbers.[4]

In the lists for Orléans were the ancient authors Homer, Virgil, Claudian, Donatus, Priscian, all led by Grammar. Ovid brought up the rear guard. For Paris Logic was the leader and by his side "civil law rode gorgeously and canon law rode haughtily." The principal champions were the scholars Plato and Aristotle. As the battle began Donatus struck Plato with a verse, which Plato parried with a sophism. Aristotle and Priscian tangled in the mêlée. By deploying Ovid's rear guard, which included Bernard Sylvester, Grammar won an early advantage, but in the end the overwhelming forces of Logic carried the day. When the dust of battle had subsided,

Grammar withdrew
Into Egypt, where she was born.
But Logic is now in vogue,
Every boy runs her course
Ere he has passed his fifteenth year;
Logic is now for children![5]

Orléans and the tradition of grammar were banished. Paris and Logic were the victors!

In the first half of the twelfth century a few masters studied the quadrivium, which directed their attention towards questions of natural philosophy. At that time the preeminent authority for the origin and nature of the universe was Plato, whose *Timaeus* survived partly in an incomplete Latin translation and partly in other Latin resumés. William of Conches composed glosses to the *Timaeus,* and with Bernard Sylvester and Thierry of Chartres he attempted to accommodate the Biblical account of creation with Plato's cosmology. By teaching that the universe was orderly and harmonious, that

[4] Translated by Louis John Paetow, *Memoirs of the University of California* IV (1) (1914), pp. 37–39.
[5] *Ibid.,* p. 59.

it was fashioned after a supreme model, that it operated independently according to innate principles, Plato encouraged the
scholars of the twelfth century to regard nature as a subject suitable
for investigation.

While this Platonic view of the universe attracted the attention
of Latin scholars, Aristotle's conception of nature was hidden from
western Europe. Since only his logical works had been translated
into Latin by 1150, his influential studies on natural science, metaphysics, and ethics were unavailable to the scholars of the West.
This truncated awareness of Aristotle's full achievement, however,
was not shared by the Muslims of the Near East, Africa, and Spain,
who had discovered most of his writings since the early Middle
Ages, translated them into Arabic, and studied them industriously.
Through contacts with Islam in the crusades and commerce of the
second half of the twelfth century, the western Latins became increasingly aware of these other facets of the Greek philosopher. In
Spain and Sicily at the frontiers between Christendom and Islam
translations were made from Arabic of the remaining works. Between 1160 and 1200 western scholars acquired the complete body
of Aristotle's writings in rough Latin versions. In the following
century most of these original translations were compared directly
with the Greek text to improve accuracy. Accompanying these new
texts were the commentaries of Muslim philosophers who had
studied Aristotle and interpreted his thought. Chief among these
was Ibn Roshd (d. 1198), known to the Latins as Averroës, who
worked in Muslim Spain. Because Averroës' esteem for Aristotle
knew no limits, he attempted to restore his system of thought to
its original purity free from Platonic influence. Although his efforts
were not entirely successful, Averroës' commentaries were translated into Latin and were considered by many as the most authentic
interpretation of the Greek philosopher.

Fully exposed to the Latin scholar of the early thirteenth
century, Aristotle was an exhaustively encyclopedic writer. His
many works covered the whole spectrum of Greek science and
philosophy: physics, botany, zoology, astronomy, logic, metaphysics, epistemology, ethics, and politics—to mention only the
most prominent. To each of these subjects he contributed his characteristic skills of systematic inquiry, precise definition, and orderly
classification. Aristotle was the classifier and organizer *par excellence.*
In particular he clarified and emphasized the tendency of ancient
Greek philosophy towards naturalism and rationalism. Aristotle
considered the world as a vast natural organism which operated
independently under its own principles. By free exercise of reason,
the human mind could penetrate the universe and understand its
essential functions. In the opinion of Averroës and his most en-
thusiastic devotees, Aristotle's philosophy represented the full

potentialities of the free exercise of natural reason. Revealed in his full measure, Aristotle confronted Latin Christendom with the authentic force of the pagan Greek intellect and precipitated a crisis.

The appearance of the new and complete Aristotle coincided with the formative period of the medieval universities. The reaction of the university masters towards the Greek philosopher became the crucial issue. Aristotle's *Ethics* was quickly inscribed on the curriculum for the Paris faculty of arts, but his metaphysical and natural works provoked sharp opposition. In 1210 a church council forbade the public or private reading of his natural philosophy and its commentaries at Paris under penalty of excommunication. Five years later when the prohibition was renewed, the restriction applied only to public reading or lecturing. In other words, the natural and metaphysical treatises were not suitable as texts for instruction, although their private reading was not hindered. Apparently, influential theologians at Paris felt that the naturalistic and rationalistic features of Aristotle's thought were irreconcilable with the supernatural character of Christian faith. Although the Papacy confirmed this condemnation of Aristotle at the beginning, in 1231 it allowed the suspected works to be corrected by a committee of scholars. By mid-century the prohibition became ineffective, and the condemned writings were openly included in the arts curriculum. The process which led to the reversal and final acceptance of the complete Aristotle by the Papacy and university authorities was the work of numerous masters at Paris, among whom certain Dominican scholars played a prominent role, as we shall see. Since Aristotle was considered the epitome of new science, many were fearful that neglect or hostility would lead to obscurantism. Others welcomed Aristotle as an exciting inspiration to reinvigorate the arts curriculum. Once his works were enrolled among the basic texts, the masters of arts enthusiastically began to gloss them in their lectures. In the thirteenth century Aristotle became the great authority for the faculty of arts.

Among the hundreds of masters who taught at Paris we may focus our attention on the figure of Siger of Brabant (d. c.1284), who served as a hero and leader in the faculty of arts during the second half of the thirteenth century. While neither his turbulent life nor his tragic ending was typical, nonetheless we can discern facets of his career which were representative of his faculty. Originating from the populous lowlands, as indicated by his name, Siger came to Paris in the 1250's to study the arts, supported by a benefice from Liège. About six years later he received his master's degree, and as was characteristic of Siger's career, the historical documents first record him involved in a violent disturbance of the faculty of arts. Siger held his classes on the Left Bank near the Seine on the rue du Fouarre (straw), so-called because the students sat on straw scattered on the floor. His teaching attracted the admiration of colleagues and the enthusiasm of a large student following. Almost all of his writings consist of *reportationes* from his lectures on the basic arts texts, and his disputations. Siger of Brabant was one of those Parisian masters who found the new Aristotle and his Arabic interpreter Averroës an exciting source of inspiration. Since Aristotle represented the full intellectual potentialities of natural reason, he became so devoted to the Greek philosopher that he was willing to follow him into philosophic doctrines contradictory of Christian tenets. We shall see that Siger's position, known as Latin Averroism, has important relevance to the problem of faith and reason. Because of his tenacious consistency, he stirred up a storm of controversy at Paris, of which he himself was the chief victim. His academic career was ended by official condemnation of the bishop of Paris in 1277, and his life was later taken by a demented secretary, but his memory was evoked in the following century when the poet Dante envisioned Siger of Brabant in Paradise at the side of Thomas Aquinas and in the company of the great Christian thinkers:

This is the eternal light of Siger
Who, when he lectured on the rue du Fouarre,
Syllogized unwelcomed truths.

(Paradiso X)

Medicine

Since ancient times the majority of men who professionally treated the sick were without formal and theoretical medical training, but were simply medical craftsmen who learned their skills as apprentices to other practitioners. Only a relatively small number received an education in a school, which might qualify them as medical doctors. In addition to the profession there were a few others who also studied medicine as part of the liberal arts. In general this legacy of Antiquity persisted into medieval times but with the introduction of one new element. In the early Middle Ages both the practice and the teaching of medicine increasingly became the monopoly of the monks. Since monasteries possessed most of the hospitals and schools they dominated medical practice. In the twelfth century, however, when the monks began to release their hold on education, they also abandoned medicine.

By the thirteenth century the two prominent centers for teaching medicine were located at Salerno to the south of Naples and Montpellier to the west of Marseilles. Some historians have derived significance from their common location on the Mediterranean since the beneficial climate promoted health resorts at Salerno, and the nearness of the Muslims influenced medical theory at Montpellier. Although Salerno was the older, extending back into the tenth century as a medical center, it was chiefly known for its practitioners. Evidence of medical education there does not appear until the twelfth century, and university organization appeared in the mid-thirteenth century. On the other hand, Montpellier can claim to be the first European medical university because its organization can be documented since 1220. Under the influence of Arabic writings the professors at Montpellier preferred a more theoretical approach to medicine. Other universities supported medical faculties of lesser rank. For example, Bologna's specialty was surgery and anatomy, and by the end of the century Paris' small faculty gained some encouragement from the Aristotelian revival. As in ancient times, most medical practitioners were without benefit of this instruction.

Medical education in the thirteenth century clearly followed the scholastic techniques developed in the universities. The standard authorities were the Greek physicians Hippocrates and Galen, to which were added the medical works of the Persian Ibn Sînâ (d. 1037), known in Latin as Avicenna, who was also a renowned commentator on Aristotle. Since the masters of Salerno and Montpellier lectured chiefly on these basic texts, their writings exist mainly in the form of commentaries. We have certain evidence of progress in medical education when in the twelfth century some medical doctors began to call themselves physicians to be distinguished from the majority of medical practitioners. This designation comes from the Greek and is related to the term physics or natural science. By adopting the title of physician the medical doctor indicated the relevance of science to his learning. In the thirteenth century the bond between medicine and science was further strengthened by the contributions of Aristotle. For example, Urso of Calabria (d. 1225), one of the outstanding professors at Salerno, made use of Aristotle's scientific works in his commentaries. Despite this progress, however, advancement in medical science did not keep pace with the other disciplines, and western medical achievements in the Middle Ages never surpassed those of the Muslims.

Law

In the thirteenth century a number of universities boasted Roman and canon law faculties, but leadership in legal science undoubtedly belonged to Bologna. At Paris, for example, the professors of canon law suffered from the absence of Romanist colleagues, who were barred from the city by the Papacy at the beginning of the century. Elsewhere Roman law was taught at Montpellier, and especially at Orléans, which offered Bologna its only real competition at the end of the century. Bologna's legal traditions went back to the turn of the eleventh century. Although obscured by the legendary haze of the remote past, the origins of Roman and canon law there were associated with two figures. Irnerius (d. 1130?), a former master of arts and a judge, taught Roman law in the neighborhood of San Stefano and composed some minor treatises and a great number of legal glosses. Somewhat later and at the opposite end of the city, Gratian (d. before 1159?), a Camaldulensian monk, taught canon law at San Felice and San Nabore and compiled an important collection of ecclesiastical law known as the *Decretum*. In their respective disciplines both men inspired students who revered their memory and who transmitted instruction for generations. For example, Irnerius' four most prominent students, Bulgarus, Martianus, Hugo and Jacobus, were called the "Four Doctors." In the third generation Bulgarus was succeeded by Johannes Bassianus and Martianus by Placentinus. Gratian's direct students probably included Rolandus Bandinelli, but in the second half of the twelfth century Rufinus and Huguccio were the most celebrated canonists. By and large the Romanists were drawn principally from Italy and were laymen who frequently bequeathed their positions to their sons. On the other hand, the canonists were more usually clerics who came to Bologna from all parts of Europe. As indicated by their names—Alanus Anglicus, Johannes Teutonicus, Laurentius Hispanus—English, Germans, Spaniards, Welsh, Hungarians, and Italians worked as an international team to create a universal ecclesiastical jurisprudence. Beginning as students, these canonists became masters and were frequently rewarded with appointments to the prelacy, sometimes as elevated as the papal throne. Rufinus and Huguccio, for example, became bishops of Assisi and Pisa respectively, and Rolandus Bandinelli was elected to the Papacy as Pope Alexander III. Churchmen fully realized the advantages of legally trained administrators. In the beginning the instruction of Roman and canon law was usually kept separate, but the advantages of interchange soon became obvious. Eventually students followed courses in both disciplines, and Johannes Faventinus was one of the first to earn the title of "Doctor of both laws."

The initial problem for the formation of legal science was the assembling of authoritative legal texts, but for the Romanists this task had been performed long ago. In the sixth century the Emperor Justinian at Constantinople had ordered the compilation of all Roman law into four major books: the Institutes (an elementary legal manual), the Digest (a collection of legal interpretations of the great classical jurists), the Code (legislation), and the *Novellae* (new laws). The total collection was known as the *Corpus iuris civilis* and embodied the highest expression of the Roman legal genius for centuries. With the decay of the Roman Empire and the barbarization of the early Middle Ages, however, the practice and instruction of Roman legal science declined markedly in western Europe. In general, Justinian's compilation fell into disuse, and in particular, the Digest, containing jurisprudence too difficult for barbaric times, was rarely copied. By rediscovering the Digest and by rehabilitating the *Corpus iuris civilis*, Irnerius made a significant recovery for Roman law at the turn of the eleventh century. From this date the principal authority for the Romanists was fully available for study and lecturing.

The canonists, on the other hand, were not so favored as the Romanists with a ready-made text. Their basic elements, such as the canons of church councils, the decretals of popes, the opinions of the Church Fathers, and the laws of secular princes, lay scattered in numerous collections from the fourth through the eleventh centuries. In irregular and often imperfect fashion these early compilations preserved and transmitted this material for canonical jurisprudence, but no one heretofore had attempted to bring it all together. When Gratian, therefore, assembled the most comprehensive collection of laws, he was in effect bringing ecclesiastical jurisprudence abreast of Justinian. His *Decretum* (c. 1140), as it was most commonly known, gave to successive canon lawyers their authoritative text for both litigation and instruction. But the contents of church law was hardly as stationary as that of Roman law. As a functioning institution, the medieval church continued to create law through councils and popes. In the twelfth and thirteenth centuries popes such as Alexander III and Innocent III were particularly active in publishing new laws. As the supreme judge of the church, the pope was responsible for judging cases with the advice of his legal experts and formulating decisions known as decretals, which provided precedents for church law. At the end of the twelfth and the beginning of the thirteenth centuries new collections were made of this material. By 1234 all was finally consolidated in a compilation authorized by Pope Gregory IX and known as the *Decretales*, to which Pope Boniface VIII made additions at the end of the century. Thus the *Decretales* were added to the *Decretum* to form the authoritative texts of canon law.

Once the authorities were established, the next step was to understand and coordinate them into a coherent juridical system. Academically this function was performed by lectures on the texts, which were transcribed in the form of glosses. The Romanists were often called glossators because they produced masses of comments on Justinian. In the beginning Irnerius' glosses were concise, brief explanations of the text, reminiscent of the early grammatical glosses with which he was familiar as a master of arts. In time the Romanist comments increased in length and sophistication. Canonists such as Rufinus and Huguccio who lectured on Gratian's *Decretum* composed similar commentaries. Eventually these glosses were assembled in an apparatus to the text, in which each author drew heavily on his predecessors' and colleagues' contributions. In effect, these legal commentaries were fully cooperative enterprises. Certain apparatuses came to be widely accepted in the schools. Designated as the *Glossae ordinariae*, they were the official commentaries to be read immediately after the text by the professor in the ordinary or regular lecture. For example, in the second quarter of the thirteenth century the Romanist Accursius (d. 1263) assembled more than 96,000 items of preceding glossators. His vast apparatus to the whole *Corpus* of Justinian was recognized as the *Glossa ordinaria* throughout the Middle Ages. Similarly Johannes Teutonicus and later Bartholomew of Brescia compiled the *Glossa ordinaria* to Gratian, and Bernard of Parma's apparatus to the *Decretales* of Gregory IX achieved the same distinction.

The compiling of authoritative texts with their glosses was closely connected with lecturing, but this procedure could only initiate and not perfect the science of jurisprudence. After the law texts had been gathered, they had to be placed in a systematic and orderly arrangement. When scholars compared laws which originated in different times and circumstances but were now set side by side, they discovered discrepancies and even clear contradictions. Since the conflicting texts produced questions to be resolved, the technique of reconciling and harmonizing them was known as "questioning." In a sense the task of questioning was already performed for the Roman law glossators. The Justinian compilers not only arranged the laws in systematic order, but they also attempted to eliminate contradictions by interpolations, or verbal alterations and insertions in the text.

For the younger science of canon law the requirements of questioning were yet to be worked out. At the turn of the eleventh century a few early canonists, sensing the need to question and to harmonize discrepancies within church law, proposed principles which the theologians also adopted. Gratian's *Decretum* finally perfected the procedures of both the canonists and theologians. Gratian arranged the material systematically according to subject matter, regardless of conflicting points. Unlike the ancient Roman jurisprudents, he made no attempt to alter the legal text by interpolation. His chief method for reconciling contradictions followed the rules of dialectics or logic. He investigated the authenticity of the texts, the context of the laws, the divergent circumstances of time, place or person which might explain discrepancies. He distinguished between general measures and particular cases, between exceptions, strict rules and counsels for perfection. Most important he examined closely the diverse meaning of words. After noting the pros and cons of each particular question, he proposed a solution entitled the "statement of Gratian." It is significant that the original title of his great compilation was the "Concordance of Discordant Canons."

Gratian's *Decretum* encompassed a wide variety of church affairs, but one question which is of interest to scholastic culture might serve to illustrate his method: Shall priests be acquainted with profane literature or not? (First Part, Distinction XXXVII).[6] On the negative side, he collected an ancient canon from a Carthaginian council which decreed that a bishop should not read the books of the heathen, and four passages from the Church Father Jerome which drew special attention to the dangers of dialectics for Christians. A final text made allusion to Jerome's famous dream in which he was chastised for being a Ciceronian. "From all of which instances," Gratian concluded, "it would seem that knowledge of profane literature is not to be sought by churchmen." "But on the other hand," he continued, "one reads that Moses and Daniel were learned in all the wisdom of the Egyptians and Chaldeans. One reads also that God ordered the sons of Israel to spoil the Egyptians of their gold and silver; the moral interpretation of this teaches that should we find in the poets either the gold of wisdom or the silver of eloquence, we should turn it to the profit of useful learning." After relating the well-known argument of "despoiling the Egyptians," Gratian collected five texts from the Church Fathers, including Jerome, and two from the popes which stressed the usefulness of pagan learning for correctly understanding the Bible. Among them Pope Clement maintained: "For when each one has learned from divine Scriptures a sound and firm rule of truth, it will not be strange if from the common culture and liberal studies, which perhaps he touched upon in his youth, he should also bring something to the support of true doctrine." At one point Gratian interjected this comment: "Then why are those writings forbidden to be read which it is shown so reasonably, should be read? While some read profane literature for their pleasure . . . , others learn them to add to their knowledge . . . that they may turn to the service of sacred and devout learning the useful things they find therein. Such are praiseworthy in adding to their learning profane literature." At the end of the question Gratian reinforced this position by concluding: "As therefore is evident from the authorities already quoted ignorance [of profane literature] ought to be odious to priests." By dialectical harmonizing of contradictory texts Gratian justified the liberal arts which, in fact, provided the techniques for effecting this reconciliation.

The Romanists further applied the questioning method to legal science in literature known as the *Summa*. Organized according to the topical plan of Justinian's Code, they were not mere glosses, but systematic and comprehensive treatises which followed the

[6]The question has been translated in Arthur O. Norton, *Readings in the History of Education: Medieval Universities* (Cambridge, Mass., 1909), pp. 60–75.

logical order of doctrine rather than the literal order of the text. In these *summae* full and reasoned discussion of the major legal topics could be found. Canonists such as Huguccio also used the *summa* technique in their commentaries to the *Decretum* and the *Decretales,* which they occasionally combined with the literal approach. These *summae,* formed by the application of dialectics to law, provided a rational synthesis of jurisprudence.

Questioning consisted of pitting one text against another in a dialectical debate among authorities to discover the truth. The element of debate is also fundamental to law practice, in which all decisions are attained from opposing arguments of contending parties. It is not surprising, therefore, that the Romanists of Bologna were the first to develop the procedure of disputation. Early in the twelfth century Bulgarus and Martianus, Irnerius' major disciples, formed rival parties of legal doctrine. Debating points of law, they produced the "Dissensions of the Masters," which recorded their conflicting opinions. Moreover, their own students performed fictitious legal disputes adjudicated by the masters. The notes of these mock trials taken by officially designated reporters in the classroom of Bulgarus are the earliest *questiones disputatae* that we possess. Originating from the contentious nature of legal science, the disputation passed from the Roman lawyers of Bologna to the canonists and the theologians. In the Middle Ages the study of law, like other disciplines, began with the reading of authoritative texts which raised questions to which solutions were reached by disputation.

By the middle of the twelfth century the Bolognese lawyers devised their basic tools, so that the thirteenth century brought forth no startling innovations in legal science, but rather the perfecting of existing techniques. A look at two of the outstanding legal masters will give us an impression of the tenor of that age. None of these representatives may be considered typical—indeed, they are known to us because of their unusual accomplishments—but in their careers we may again discern the characteristics of their profession. In mid-thirteenth-century Bologna the most successful of all Romanist professors was Accursius (d. 1263). A Florentine by birth he studied at Bologna and could trace his academic pedigree through Johannes Bassianus and Bulgarus to Irnerius. He himself enjoyed a fruitful career as professor at Bologna for about forty years, and his major work was the *Glossa ordinaria,* as we have seen. Prior to Accursius most glossators limited their attention to the Code, but his significant contribution was to provide an extensive apparatus for Justinian's entire *Corpus iuris civilis.* Although relatively little of his work was original, he nonetheless made available in convenient form the great wealth of Roman law scholarship to others. Because of this apparatus Accursius was known to later Romanists as the "idol of the glossators," but his success is also indicated by other tangible signs. His marriage was fruitful in a number of sons who followed his footsteps into the legal profession. The most famous was Francesco, who was also a celebrated master at Bologna, but whose subsequent reputation was blemished when Dante depicted him among the sodomites in Hell (*Inferno XV*). As a prominent citizen of Bologna, the father Accursius was active in the communal government, and the son Francesco served King Edward I of England. Furthermore, the teaching of law and political service carried material rewards, indicated by Accursius' fine town house on the central public square and his gracious country villa. This professor of Roman law could have provided no better symbol of his social position and wealth at Bologna than the magnificent tomb, which he shared with Francesco, located to this day behind the church of San Francesco (Plate I). Within and without this church and also at San Domenico are equally splendid tombs of contemporary glossators. Indeed, so exalted was the status of these legists in the thirteenth century that they exchanged their master's degree for the title of "lord of the laws."

Henry of Susa (d. 1271), or Hostiensis, as he was later known, was of comparable stature among the thirteenth-century canonists. Originating from the neighborhood of Turin, Henry pursued his studies in both Roman and canon law at Bologna, where he earned the degree of Doctor of Both Laws. While it is likely that he taught for a short time at Bologna, his major professorial career was at Paris, where he lectured in canon law. Despite this sojourn in France, he was Bolognese at heart, for in his last testament he bequeathed his books to the school in which he was nurtured. Henry of Susa produced two major works, both based on the *Decretales* of Gregory IX: his *Lectura*, a voluminous commentary resulting from his Paris lectures, and a monumental *Summa*, his most important writing. Although this last book followed the organization of the *Decretales*, it exceeded the glosses of the *Lectura* and discussed canon law in the comprehensive and logical fashion of the Romanist tradition. Furthermore, Henry introduced in his canon law the contributions of Roman law wherever pertinent, so that his *Summa* became equally important for the development of both laws. A *summa* in the fullest sense, his work synthesized both Roman and ecclesiastical jurisprudence, and we shall see that it was a worthy counterpart of the contemporary theological *summae*. When the book was known in later times as the *Golden Summa*, Henry's reputation as a great canonist was assured. Renown in legal scholarship also brought opportunities of political service and reward. Soon after performing missions for the Papacy and King Henry III of England, Henry was named bishop of Sisteron, later transferred to the archbishopric of Embrun, and was finally elevated to the cardinal-bishopric of Ostia (hence his later name of Hostiensis). Just as

Accursius had achieved wealth and social prestige, so Henry of Susa attained advancement in the church through mastery of legal science. In medieval times, as today, the legal profession as a whole was often accused of motives of vainglory and greed, and individual men of stature were exposed to criticism which insinuated these vices. When the poet Dante (*Paradiso XII*) alludes to the great canonist Hostiensis, we find an echo of this innuendo.

The academic feud depicted by Henry of Andeli in his *Battle of the Seven Arts* involved Romanists, canonists and medical doctors as well as masters of arts, but

Madame la Haute Science [*Lady Theology*],
Who did not care a fig about their dispute,
Left the arts to fight it out together.
Methinks she went to Paris
To drink the wines of her cellar.[1]

This aloofness which the poet perceived was engendered by the theologians' high regard for their profession. On the authority of the early Church Fathers, they viewed the liberal arts as handmaidens or preparatory disciplines for their subject. Law and medical science were disdained as the lucrative studies. They alone strove for the highest wisdom possible to man, the knowledge of God which encompassed and gave perspective to all other learning. In the Middle Ages theology was the queen of the faculties. Although the lawyers might demur at these superior attitudes, most others would probably have conceded the theologian's high esteem. Theology was a disinterested discipline, which led less directly to wealth or influence than medicine and law. Comprising knowledge valued for its own sake, it attracted the best intellects of the day. Without doubt the medieval genius was expressed in theology.

When in the early twelfth century Abelard had satisfied his curiosity for dialectics and philosophy, he turned to theology as a new realm to conquer. By common consensus the city of Laon, lying to the northeast of Paris, was the foremost center for sacred science. He went there, attended the lectures of the renowned theologian, Anselm of Laon, and returned to Paris loudly maintaining that Anselm's reputation was grossly overrated. "When he

THEOLOGY: THE QUEEN OF THE FACULTIES

[1] Translated by Louis John Paetow, *Memoirs of the University of California* IV(1) (1914), 43.

lit the torch of learning," Abelard declared, "he only filled the room with smoke." In an effort to rival Laon, Abelard began teaching theology at Paris. Partly because of his talent for exciting followers, but mainly because of advantages which we have seen, Paris surpassed Laon as a theological center by the middle of the twelfth century. From then on the theological faculty at Paris was preeminent in western Europe. If Laon had been known for its Anselm, soon after, Paris boasted an international cluster of masters, each of whom drew a following of students. The Breton Abelard himself (d. 1142) brought disciples to the schools of Notre-Dame and Saint-Geneviève as well as into the countryside of Champagne. The German Hugh (d. 1141) attracted pupils to the abbey of Saint-Victor on the Left Bank. Gilbert de la Porrée (d. 1154), originally from Poitou, left his Chancellorship at Chartres to teach theology at Paris before he became bishop of his native town, and Peter the Lombard (d. 1160), later bishop of Paris, filled the teaching posts at Notre-Dame with his disciples for the rest of the century. In the age of the individual master these theologians were able to impress the stamp of their salient ideas on their disciples and to create what might be called schools of thought. Since their writings often consisted of *reportationes,* it became increasingly difficult to distinguish the master from his students within the school. Many theological treatises, for example, can only be ascribed to the school of Abelard or that of Gilbert. This underlying importance of schools of thought continued into the thirteenth century when they became increasingly institutionalized. Because of the succession of masters and students at the Cordeliers, we can discern a Franciscan school of theological thought, which included the Englishman Alexander of Hales (d. 1245) and the Italian Bonaventure (d. 1274). The Dominicans at Saint-Jacques likewise produced a coherent school, numbering among their most illustrious the German Albert the Great (d. 1280) and the Italian Thomas Aquinas (d. 1274). Even the arts scholars at Paris formed a school of secular masters, exemplified by Siger of Brabant (d. 1284), whose discussions were relevant to theological problems. Much of the intellectual controversy of the thirteenth century was generated by these schools.

The Problem of Authority in Theology

Despite their superior airs, the theologians profited from developments in the other disciplines. Particularly with the masters of arts and lawyers they shared the common problems and solutions of the schools, so that their own history ran parallel with the others in applying the scholastic method to theology. As in all learning, theological study began with authority, which, in this case, was the Bible. The Old and New Testaments were the fundamental source of the unique ideas of the Christian religion. Here, for example, the theologian derived his conception that God is one being but three persons (doctrine of the Trinity); that at a certain point in time God created the world out of nothing by His own voluntary act (doctrine of Creation); that man, created perfectly by God, chose to rebel against his Maker and thereby fell into sin (doctrine of the Fall); that God sent His Son Jesus Christ into the world to restore fallen man by grace (doctrine of the Incarnation); that Christ instituted the church and the sacraments as means to provide this grace to the world (doctrine of the church); and that Christ will come again at the end of the ages to judge the world and usher in His Kingdom (doctrine of the last judgment). As we shall see, although some theologians held that the ancient Greek philosophers had an oblique notion of these doctrines through natural reason, all theologians did agree the scriptures constituted the clearest source of these uniquely Christian conceptions. In other words, the theologians maintained that God revealed Himself most fully in the Bible and that this knowledge must be accepted by faith. Because God Himself was the author, the Scriptures were authoritative for theology in a more absolute sense than the fallible texts of other disciplines.

Since theology began with Scriptural study, theologians designated themselves as masters of the sacred page in the early twelfth century. At that time the foremost center for Biblical study at Paris was the abbey of Saint-Victor under the inspiration of its prior, Hugh. Following the lead of the Church Fathers, the Victorines perfected the medieval method of interpreting the Scriptures according to three different approaches: history, allegory and morality. First they examined the literal meaning of the text to discover the historical facts. Then they searched for symbolic significance beyond these literal facts. When a figurative interpretation yielded theological doctrine, this interpretation was called allegory; when it produced ethical precepts, it was designated morality. For example, historically interpreted, the Old Testament figure Job was the ancient Hebrew patriarch of the Biblical narrative. Allegorically, he symbolized Christ, who left His former glory to suffer the miseries of the world, and morally, he signified any sort of just or spiritual penance. This threefold method of Scriptural study also utilized different scholarly disciplines. The literal method employed the skills of grammar and chronology to aid the historian, while the other two made use of logic to provide illustrations of right faith for the theologian in allegory and examples of good conduct for the preacher in morality. Although the Victorines used all three levels of Scriptural interpretation, they especially emphasized the literal or historical approach. To them Christ's religion was not so much based on logic as on facts registered in history, and therefore, theology should be studied essentially as a historical problem. The Victorines set an example for succeeding theologians by composing a large literature of Biblical commentaries according to the three levels of interpretation. This glossing of the Scriptures became standard procedure for training candidates for the degree of master of theology. In the mid-thirteenth century one of the prescribed stages in the theological course was the Biblical Bachelor, an advanced student who lectured on two books of the Scriptures for two years.

The Scriptural scholar in the Middle Ages was not free to interpret his subject according to his fancy, but was required to take account of past interpretations, particularly by those who were revered as the Fathers of the church. These Church Fathers, who included Ambrose (d. 397), Jerome (d. 420), Augustine (d. 430) and Pope Gregory the Great (d. 604), wrote voluminously on all aspects of Christian faith and life. Because of their acknowledged sanctity and forceful intellects, their writings assumed authority supplementary, if not equal, to that of the Bible. To interpret the Scriptures rightly the scholar was compelled to consult patristic opinion, but several problems faced the theologian of the twelfth century seeking to make use of this material. Because of its massive quantity and its wide dispersion through many works, he needed both to assemble it from the various authors and to organize it systematically. At the start, the theologian faced problems similar to those of the canonist. Although these tasks had been approached sporadically during the early Middle Ages, the school of Laon at the beginning of the twelfth century was the first to make a concerted effort to deal with them seriously. Under the leadership of Anselm of Laon these theologians organized the patristic material according to the arrangement of the Bible. To this end they produced a short commentary on the whole Scriptures composed of a mosaic of patristic opinion, which was accepted in the schools as the *Glossa ordinaria.* During the Biblical lectures of the thirteenth century then, this gloss was normally read along with the sacred text. Moreover, the school of Laon began to organize the material of the Church Fathers logically and systematically according to doctrinal themes in compilations called *Books of Sentences.* (The term "sentence" simply meant the opinion of a Father.) Performing the humble but necessary service of collecting and classifying the patristic authorities essential for theological study, Anselm and his followers prepared the texts for the lecture halls.

Once the theological authorities were collected, read, and classified, difficulties began to emerge quite like those of canon law. Inconsistancies cropped up within the Bible. Passages of one Father appeared to contradict those of another or even disagreed with his other opinions. Sometimes the Fathers seemed to be at variance even with the Scriptures. The theologian's next task was to pose questions to harmonize his authoritative texts. Although the canonists, as we have seen, were the first to sense these difficulties at the end of the eleventh century, they were shortly followed by the theologians such as Abelard whose contributions in turn were incorporated by Gratian. Canonists and theologians, therefore, developed a common method of questioning. Abelard approached the problem directly by listing 168 questions on which he had found divergent authoritative opinion. They ranged from crucial ones such as "Should God be believed in?" to "Is it permissible to lie?" He then collected all authoritative texts he could find pro and con each question and thus named his book *Sic et Non* (For and Against). Since it was impossible for Abelard to have read exhaustively all the authors he quoted, he was forced to rely on the *Books of Sentences* of Laon, which he had disdained so publicly. His purpose was not to cast doubt or ridicule on conflicting authorities in the manner of a skeptic, as some have seen it; rather Abelard stated plainly that he merely wished to challenge his readers to reconcile the authorities through dialectical reasoning. For this purpose he set down in the preface rules for harmonizing these conflicts. Similar to the canonists, he investigated authenticity and context and distinguished the different kinds of precepts. Of greatest importance, as we shall see, he proposed that the various meanings of conflicting words be carefully examined. This close analysis of terminology required the cooperation of grammar and logic.

Since Abelard provided no solutions for the questions he raised but only the method for arriving at them, we may regard his work as a manual of exercises or a book of problems for theological students. To offer answers to these questions was the next obvious step, and this is precisely what Peter the Lombard accomplished in his *Four Books of Sentences*. Peter posed the questions, assembled the authorities for and against, and attempted a solution. While his conclusions were not always too convincing, the Lombard's chief contributions were the organization and logical arrangement of all the questions according to topics such as the Trinity, Creation, Incarnation, and Sacraments. As demonstrated in Peter's work, theology eventually became detached from Bible study and began to follow independently the logic of its doctrines. Scriptural revelation still provided the contents, but no longer the sole organizational framework. The *Sentences* of Peter the Lombard became a new authoritative text for teaching in the schools. Like so many textbooks it was not a work of genius, but it was popular because it provided basic information usefully arranged. Theological masters soon began to give lectures and produce commentaries on the *Sentences*, and by the mid-thirteenth century the theological course at Paris included the Bachelor of Sentences, an advanced student who followed directly after the Bachelor of Bible, and who lectured on the Lombard for one year.

Under the influence of the lawyers, the theologians during the second half of the twelfth century also conducted disputations, which simply institutionalized the *questio* technique in the schools. By the thirteenth century the theological masters and bachelors at Paris regularly practiced both the *questiones disputatae* and the *disputationes de quolibet* of which a great number of determinations have survived. Moreover, the rediscovery of Aristotle's *Topics* and *Sophistic Refutations* around the middle of the twelfth century gave to the theologians as well as the other scholars precise regulations for conducting arguments and debates. Aristotle's complete logical treatises, therefore, set the ground rules for disputations. Disputation had become so important in the thirteenth century that it began to influence the modes of expression of theological literature. Masterpieces such as the *Summa theologica* of Thomas Aquinas or the *Commentary to the Sentences* of Bonaventure were not divided into chapters but into units called articles, which treated a single doctrinal point and followed a set pattern of exposition. The subject of the article was phrased as a question to provoke discussion. The author marshalled authorities opposing the question, and then followed with another series of texts which presented an alternative to the first series and which suggested his solution. Having stated his own conclusion, the author finally sought to answer the first series of opposing arguments. In the dialectic of pros and cons the scholastic theologian attempted to resolve the conflicts among the authorities and thereby to discover the truth. In effect the article was simply the formalized expression of a master's determination of a theological disputation.

The disputation, however, treated only a limited question and did not relate its specific resolution to the rest of theology. By the middle of the thirteenth century scholars recognized that the Biblical *lectio* and the theological *disputatio* were unable to provide a comprehensive organization for divine science. In the preface to his *Breviloquium,* Bonaventure noted: "These truths are so widely diffused throughout the works of saints and doctors that they could not all be read or heard by Scriptural students even in a long time. Beginners in this study of theology, in fact, often dread the Scripture itself, feeling it to be confusing, orderless, and uncharted as some impenetrable forest."[2] In the introduction to his *Summa theologica,* Thomas Aquinas elaborated this theme: "For we have observed that beginners in this doctrine have been considerably hampered by what various authors have written. They have been hampered partly because of the multiplication of useless questions, articles, and arguments; partly, too, they have been hampered because those things that are needful for them to know are not taught according

[2]Translated in Guy J. Bougerol, *Introduction to the Works of Bonaventure* (Paterson, N. J., 1964), pp. 108, 109.

to the order of the subject matter, but rather according as the order of exposition in books demands, or according as the occasion for disputation arises; and partly they have been hampered because frequent repetition brought about weariness and confusion in the minds of readers."[3] Dialectics, therefore, could provide a further service to theologians by suggesting a method of organization. As in law, theology began to depart from the simple reading of the authoritative text, to follow the inner reason of its doctrines. Here again Aristotle the logician provided crucial help. Not only furnishing rules governing argument and debate, he also formulated a logical procedure for defining, distinguishing, and categorizing. Aristotle himself successfully applied these skills to a wide range of knowledge, and therefore bequeathed important tools for systematizing theological knowledge. Aristotle, the system builder of Antiquity, was now employed in raising a medieval edifice of theology.

Following the Romanists, who, we have seen, entitled their systematic and comprehensive treatises as *Summae*, the theologians likewise adopted the term to designate their attempts at rational organization. The outstanding example of this literature was Thomas Aquinas' *Summa theologica*, which in size and in perfection towered above all others, although it was left unfinished at his death. Thomas built his work with the building blocks of articles arranged in a vast system patterned after the ancient Greek theme of emanation and return. Since theology was divine science, all things should be studied as proceeding from and returning to God. In other words, God is both the beginning and the end of everything. The first part, therefore, dealt with God and His creation as the source of all existence, and the second with morality or God as the standard of all conduct. The third part treated the doctrine of Incarnation as the specific conditions of this return. Within this general scheme Thomas arranged the units of theological knowledge and held them in place with the mortar of Aristotle's logical definitions and categories. In this monumental edifice there was a place for everything and everything had its place.

Since it would have been impossible for a single mind, even of the brilliance of Thomas Aquinas', to have read all of the material and solved all of the problems involved in the *Summa theologica*, Thomas was dependent on the work of his predecessors. From the days of Anselm of Laon theologians were engaged in assembling the mass of theological authorities, reading and commenting on them, and attempting to master their contents. Moreover, they were busy smoothing out the conflicts between authorities and debating thorny questions. Since the end of the twelfth century innumerable

[3]Translated in A. C. Pegis, ed., *The Basic Writings of Saint Thomas Aquinas* (New York, 1945), I, p. 3.

disputations were held as a part of the academic routine. The masters made their determinations and recorded their solutions in *reportationes*. In this contentious atmosphere one master accepted, another rejected the solutions of his colleagues, but the questions were hammered out and refined in the schools. When particularly satisfactory solutions were achieved, one theologian after another adopted them and transmitted them in his writings. These medieval professors, for whom private property was not applicable to the realm of ideas, were unaware of modern notions of plagiarism. Whatever was true was the common property of all. As a master of theology at Paris, Thomas Aquinas benefited from these achievements of his fellow workers. Some articles he took directly from his predecessors with little or no change; many more he modified in one way or another; but even when he rejected his forerunners' conclusions he benefited from their debate and objections. Thomas' great contribution was to assemble all of these articles in a magnificent system, yet much of the work had already been performed. In the fullest sense the great *Summae theologicae* of the thirteenth century were created by corporations of theological masters. As cooperative enterprises, they were, in fact, products of the universities.

The Problem of Reason in Theology

A medieval theologian read and compiled the authoritative statements of the Bible and the Church Fathers, classified their concepts, coordinated their agreements and noted their conflicts. To reconcile the latter he scrutinized the texts and probed their linguistic meaning, but eventually he arrived at an impasse until he could find an outside source for criticizing his authorities. By itself authority could take him no farther. Help lay close at hand, however, in the human function of reason regulated by the laws of logic and dialectics. This alternative revived the old question of what role reason played in understanding the contents of authority. The question lay at the heart not only of Christianity but of all religions (Islam, for example) which claim divine revelation not available to ordinary human knowledge. Since the issue is fundamental, it has been controversial, and to this day, scholars have not been able to agree over its terms and conclusions. In the Christian context, however, authoritative revelation has been traditionally associated with faith. In other words, by faith an individual apprehended the special contents of revelation. It was distinguished from reason or the unaided powers of the human mind, which in the Middle Ages were associated with the logical procedures developed by the ancient Greeks. The problem of reason understanding authority was phrased as the relationship between faith and reason, but often its scope was broadened to include the conflict between Christian revelation and Greek philosophy.

In late Antiquity the question of faith and reason was boldly framed by Augustine (d. 430), the greatest of the Church Fathers. Exposing his passionately devout nature in his *Confessions*, Augustine viewed all human knowledge as essentially a dialogue between God and the soul. Not only did God reveal Himself to Christians in a special way through Christ and the Scriptures, but He also made ordinary knowledge possible to mankind. Just as light serves our physical vision, so divine illumination enables our knowing. Christ, the Word of God, is the master within each man who teaches all things that are true. To Augustine, God was the first principle of knowledge. Although we need not be concerned with the details of his theory of knowledge, it gives us insight into his solution for the problem of faith and reason. His answer was quite simple: "If you are not able to understand, believe that you might understand. Faith precedes; understanding follows." Since God is the source of knowing, it follows that faith in God is the primary condition for understanding, and no true understanding was possible without faith. Two important consequences proceeded from this formulation. In the first place faith and reason are not really distinct in Augustine's view. Since Christ is the sole teacher of mankind, He is the common source of both, but even more significant, since faith is the prerequisite for understanding, reason cannot operate apart from faith. Not only does faith supply the special truths for understanding Christian revelation, but belief in God's existence is the necessary explanation for all knowledge. Because of its crucial role, Augustine emphasized, in the second place, the primacy of faith over reason. Faith is the germinating seed of knowledge; reason and understanding are its fruits. Thus Augustine's great legacy to the Middle Ages was the formula: I believe in order that I might understand.

With few exceptions the theologians of the early Middle Ages accepted the Augustinian solution without much discussion. No significant development in the problem of faith and reason occurred until the late eleventh century when Anselm of Bec (d. 1109), whom we remember as the last genius of the monastic centuries of education, revived Augustine's formula and endowed it with an important modification. The stimulus behind Anselm's thinking was a controversy which arose over the nature of transubstantiation in the second half of the eleventh century. According to patristic authority, the doctrine of transubstantiation maintained that the elements of bread and wine of the eucharist were miraculously transformed into the actual body and blood of Christ by the consecration of the priest. The two principal antagonists of this controversy were Berengar of Tours and Lanfranc of Bec, both of whom excelled in grammar and logic. In an effort to understand this mystery of the faith Berengar applied to transubstantiation the categories of substance and accidents found in Aristotle's "old logic." The accidents were the physical appearance of the bread and wine; the substance was the miraculous presence of Christ. Since Aristotle seemed to teach that accidents cannot change without a corresponding change of substance, this would invalidate the doctrine of transubstantiation because apparently the physical appearance was not altered by the consecration. To defend the traditional doctrine Lanfranc did not revert to authority but met Berengar on his own ground. By closely examining Aristotle's categories of substance and accidents he tried to show that the physical appearance need not change to transform the reality of the eucharist. Although we need not enter into the technicalities, Lanfranc charged Berengar with misapplying Aristotle's logic. The significance of this controversy was that for the first time two theologians argued about a mystery of the faith purely in terms of grammar and dialectics. As one contemporary observed, "wherever the text lent itself to such a procedure, he [Lanfranc] based his expositions, assumptions, and conclusions on the laws of dialectics."

Originally Anselm came to Normandy to hear the lessons of Lanfranc and succeeded his master as teacher, abbot of Bec, and finally Archbishop of Canterbury. Under Lanfranc's inspiration, he composed an elementary treatise on logic entitled *De grammatico* because it began with an analysis of words. With the tools of grammar and dialectics alone he investigated the revealed mysteries of divine existence, the Trinity, Incarnation, and Atonement. The impetus of these interests and the novelty of his conclusions, as well as the controversy between Berengar and Lanfranc, encouraged him to reconsider the traditional relationship between faith and reason formulated by Augustine. With the great Church Father, Anselm shared a saintly life and devotional habits of thought. When he reopens the subject, one can hear an unmistakable echo from Augustine's *Confessions*:

Now, O Lord my God, teach my heart where and how to seek Thee, where and how to find Thee. Lord, Lord, illuminate us; show us Thyself. . . . Teach me to seek Thee and show Thyself to my search; for I cannot seek Thee unless Thou dost teach, nor find Thee unless Thou dost show Thyself. . . . I make no attempt, Lord, to penetrate Thy depths, for my intellect has no such reach; but I desire to understand some measure of Thy truth, which my heart believes and loves. I do not seek to know in order that I believe; but I believe that I may know. For I believe this also, that unless I shall have believed, I shall not understand.[4]

---

[4]Translated in Henry Osborn Taylor, *The Mediaeval Mind* (Cambridge, Mass., 1949), I, p. 278.

In his restatement of Augustine's solution, Anselm retained the essential unity between faith and reason. There is no distinction between the contents of faith and reason; both occupy the same ground. Where faith precedes, reason has the right to follow. Faith maps out the terrain, setting the boundaries. Reason comes behind, testing the area more closely. Anselm, therefore, felt perfectly free to investigate revealed doctrines with the instruments of grammar and logic. Faith is like the answers in the back of a schoolbook. When the pupil knows the correct answer, he is guided in the solution of his problems. Although faith remained the necessary condition for understanding as with Augustine, Anselm shifted the emphasis between the two elements. More concerned with the function of understanding, he expressed the kernel of his interest in the subtitle of his most influential work, the *Proslogion*—"Faith seeking understanding." Unlike Augustine he assigned primacy to reason. Eschewing the aid of the Scriptures and the Fathers, he wanted to understand as much faith as he could on rational premises. For him reason produced intelligence by two ways: by showing the interrelationship and logical coherence between concepts and by demonstrating rational necessity. With these tools Anselm penetrated the sacred precincts of theology. Doubtlessly the sanctity of his life and the reverence of his mind shielded his bold approach from censure, but Anselm was also modest in his goals. Because reason was difficult, provisional, and fallible, he was prepared that reason might not be able to follow faith all the way. As he phrased it in one of his letters, "The Christian ought to progress through faith to understanding, and not through understanding to faith. Let him rejoice if he is able to attain understanding; and if he cannot, let him revere what he cannot apprehend." [5]

Anselm's proposition of faith seeking understanding set the theological program for the twelfth century. Although the masters of the turbulent schools of Paris often lacked Anselm's reputation for piety, they nonetheless attempted to follow his intellectual ideal. Among these Abelard and Gilbert de la Porrée were the most influential. Abelard has enjoyed greater appreciation from modern historians, but during the twelfth century Gilbert commanded equal if not greater esteem. Both their careers and intellectual interests exhibit remarkable similarities, and in the fierce controversies which they generated, both were occasionally forced to modify their positions. In contrast to Anselm's reverence, Abelard has been formerly regarded as a skeptic or freethinker, but now many scholars maintain that both he and Gilbert were in fact following Anselm's example. Abelard and Gilbert fully accepted the formulations of faith contained in the Scriptures and the Fathers, but they regarded them

[5]Translated in R. W. Southern, *Saint Anselm and his Biographer* (Cambridge, 1966), p. 54.

not merely as statements to be assented to, but rather as intellectual propositions to be understood. In short, they attempted to understand what they believed. Their program was to find support for authority from reason, and the chief object of their investigations was one of the central mysteries of the Christian faith, the doctrine of the Trinity.

Since the contents of revelation were expressed in language, the appropriate instruments were grammar and logic. Like his predecessors Berengar, Lanfranc, and Anselm, Gilbert was skilled in grammar as well as in logic, and Abelard's expertise in dialectics was proverbial. Combining these two skills they undertook an analysis of theological language in general and of the Trinity in particular. Just as Abelard in his *Sic et Non* proposed to investigate words as a means for resolving contradictions, so he applied this method to the names of God in order to understand the mysteries of the Trinity. Likewise Gilbert devised a system of linguistic analysis which could be applied to all areas of thought, even theology. The basic premise of their efforts was that the language of theology bore direct correspondence to the spiritual realities which it expressed. For example, the names and attributes of God adequately revealed the divine nature. If one studied them grammatically and logically, he could obtain valid knowledge of the Godhead. Under the duress of controversy both Abelard and Gilbert were forced to admit that in the case of profound mysteries such as the Trinity a gulf might exist between reality and its verbal expression. Conceding that not all of faith could be adequately expressed in language, they realized that an investigation of language might not always lead to full understanding of faith. Despite these limitations, both Abelard and Gilbert nonetheless attempted to demonstrate the reasonableness of faith by grammar and logic. Through their efforts faith was seeking understanding. The success of their endeavors is indicated by a shift in terminology. Abelard himself gave currency to the word theology, which connoted the rational expression of God. By the middle of the twelfth century the former "master of the sacred page" was known as the "master of theology." Theology had become a fully speculative science.

As innovators the speculative theologians of the twelfth century were exposed to attacks from their conservative colleagues. For example, Abelard at his most radical moment proposed that since Christian theology was rational, then reasonable-minded men such as Socrates before the time of Christ must have known of the mystery of the Incarnation. In reply, the Victorines, to whom Christian revelation was a matter of history not of logic, protested that this was historical nonsense. The most formidable adversary of the speculative theologians was the ponderous Cistercian abbot,

Bernard of Clairvaux (d. 1153), who, we remember, expressed the new piety of the rural monasteries, and distrusted the urban schools of the secular clergy. Brandishing political as well as spiritual influence, Bernard waged an all-out campaign against Abelard and Gilbert, harassing them with letters and arraigning them before church councils. His direct accusations concerned specific theological errors, but undoubtedly the controversy touched more fundamental issues. In modern times historians have been tempted to see Bernard as the champion of dogmatic faith challenging Abelard the proponent of unfettered reason, but recent scholarship doubts that the lines were drawn so simply. Just as Abelard accepted faith, so Bernard was not unequivocally against reason. Bernard's chief objection to Abelard and Gilbert seemed to have been that they were confusing the legitimate boundaries between faith and reason. In letter after letter he protested the introduction of reason and logic into the realms of faith. Reason has its appropriate sphere of operation, but it cannot be used to profane the sanctuary of divine mystery. His objections against the use of dialectics in theology were reechoed throughout the twelfth century, but what Bernard and his followers seemed to have been proposing was a division of knowledge into two realms, the one investigated by faith, the other by reason. In effect Bernard introduced a breach into Anselm's unity of faith seeking understanding.

Whatever cleavage existed between faith and reason was further accentuated by the progressive appearance of Aristotle's works. By the middle of the twelfth century, as we have seen, Aristotle's complete system of logic was available to scholars in Paris. Not only did this dialectical science aid the theologians in reconciling conflicting authorities, constructing systems, and regulating disputations, but it also contributed to the development of speculative theology. Aristotelian logic was fully employed in the service of understanding Christian revelation. At the turn of the twelfth century a new wave of Aristotle's writings on natural science, metaphysics and morality inundated the Paris schools. Students and masters of arts eagerly acclaimed the Greek philosopher as their new authority from whom they sought fresh inspiration. Under the influence of conservative theologians, as we have seen, the first reaction of the ecclesiastical authorities was to ban the teaching of Aristotle's new works from Paris, but this precaution was only a temporary solution. Eventually the theologians were obliged to formulate a carefully considered response to the new philosophy, which the faculty of arts so loudly proclaimed, or suffer the accusation of obscurantism. The new writings of Aristotle on natural science and metaphysics fully embodied the ancient Greek conceptions of naturalism and rationalism. Some scholars of arts were even claiming that they realized the final potentialities of reason. Aristotle as reason's most skillful authority became known as "the philosopher." Not only did the general tenor of his works seem to contrast with the supernatural and nonrational characteristics of revealed Christianity, but some of his specific concepts, such as the eternal and necessary existence of the world and the impossibility of individual immortality, conflicted squarely with theological doctrine. More than ever the theologians were faced with a new and colossal authority to reconcile with Christian revelation.

At the end of the twelfth century the pressure of the new Aristotle had already widened the gap between faith and reason. At that time Simon of Tournai, a theologian at Paris, stated quite bluntly: "With Aristotle the argument is reason producing faith; whereas with Christ it is faith producing reason. Aristotle says, understand and you will believe, but Christ says, believe and you will understand." Anselm's former position was both reversed and split in two. The fundamental problem for the theologians was: What was now to be the relation between Christ and Aristotle, theology and philosophy, faith and reason? Sharply debated by the Paris theologians, this momentous question received at least three answers by the middle of the thirteenth century. The Franciscan masters Alexander of Hales and Bonaventure at the convent of the Cordeliers maintained what might be called the conservative position. Although they employed Aristotle's logical and philosophical distinctions to supplement theology, they rejected his essential authority in philosophy. By ignoring Aristotle and by renewing their allegiance to the traditions of Anselm and Augustine, the Franciscans hoped to preserve the intellectual unity of Christendom. In the debates over Aristotle at Paris, Bonaventure preached a series of sermons, one of which was significantly entitled, "Christ the teacher of all." In this he argued that Christ, who is the one universal Master, guarantees the unity of knowledge. The Franciscans denied any distinction between theology and philosophy because Christ is the source for both. Faith is the prime condition of reason and cannot be separated from it. All knowledge should be organized around Christian wisdom. In the last analysis Franciscan philosophy was essentially Augustinianism revived in the university and reexpressed in scholastic terminology.

In direct opposition to the Franciscans were the masters of the secular clergy who taught in the Paris faculty of arts. Led by Siger of Brabant they enthusiastically elevated Aristotle to their supreme authority as interpreted by Averroës' commentaries. To them Aristotle's philosophy achieved the fullest potentiality of natural reason, and was totally separate from theology, which operated according to the principle of faith. Unlike the Franciscans the

Latin Averroists envisaged a final divorce between theology and philosophy, between faith and reason. Where Aristotle specifically contradicted Christian doctrine, they felt that the conflict was unfortunate but inevitable. Although, as a Christian, Siger of Brabant might concede the higher truth of faith in such cases, he made no effort to reconcile the disparities. With the Averroists the traditional programs of reconciling authorities and of faith seeking understanding were abandoned.

A third and intermediate position between the Franciscans and the Averroists was taken by the Dominican masters Albert the Great and Thomas Aquinas at Saint-Jacques. Although Albert led the way in the Dominican school, his most brilliant student Thomas perfected his approach. With the Franciscans they wished to preserve the unity of faith and reason; with the Averroists, they recognized the undeniable genius of Aristotle. Their goal was to introduce the Greek philosopher into the Christian household of faith without precipitating a collapse. Albert's and Thomas' basic advance towards this goal was to establish a clear distinction between the sphere of theology and that of philosophy, the former which deals with supernatural phenomena by faith and the latter with natural phenomena by reason. Through practically every problem that they considered, they drew a line, assigning half to the realm of faith and the other to reason. For example, they divided the moral system into two parts composed of natural virtues, which were available to all men through reason, and supernatural virtues, which were attainable only by Christians through grace. The complete ethical code combined the cardinal virtues of Classical Antiquity, such as prudence, justice, bravery and temperance, and the theological virtues of the Scriptures, such as faith, hope, and love. We shall see that in a similar way, they distinguished between two ways of knowing God. The effect of their division was to liberate theology from philosophy and philosophy from theology with the intention of reducing the tensions between the two.

In philosophy and natural science Aristotle was the supreme authority. While Albert and Thomas did not hesitate to correct him on certain points, by and large they accepted the Greek philosopher's theories on metaphysics, physics, astronomy, and physiology as those which most reasonably approximated the truth. The Scriptures interpreted by the Church Fathers remained the uncontested authorities in theology. Accepting these by faith, the theologian gained his clearest conceptions of the supernatural world. The Dominican scholars maintained that only through divine revelation could fullest knowledge be attained of mysteries such as the Trinity, the Incarnation, and the Resurrection. Anselm, Abelard and Gilbert were mistaken, therefore, in attempting to investigate the Trinity with the tools of reason, because these particular mysteries lay exclusively in the realm of theology governed by faith. Since the division between theology and philosophy, however, was not so much one of contents as of methods of knowing, the crucial distinction between faith and reason was their divergent procedures for seeking truth. It would be possible, however, for both to occupy the same territory and to treat in common a limited number of problems from two different approaches. Among these common grounds were certain aspects of the nature of God. While some divine characteristics such as the Trinity and Incarnation could only be known through revelation, others such as the existence, unity, and power of God could also be known through philosophical reasoning. Thomas, in particular, envisaged two kinds of theology, a dogmatic theology based exclusively on revelation, and a natural theology which could be legitimately investigated by reason as well as by faith. By rational proofs, which followed suggestions found in Aristotle, the philosopher could demonstrate the existence, unity, and omnipotence of God, but at a point where reason breaks down, the theologian must carry on through faith. In effect, then, Albert and Thomas attempted to solve the problem of reason and faith by dividing it into three separate areas: that of natural philosophy, which was the exclusive province of reason, that of dogmatic theology, which was the exclusive province of faith, and an intermediate region of natural theology which was shared by both reason and faith. When Thomas treated natural science, he followed Aristotle completely, but when he spoke of God he was much more original. Freely correcting and undoubtedly surpassing the achievements of the Greek philosopher, Thomas made significant alterations in the metaphysics of Aristotle by developing his conception of God. In treating the Godhead, Thomas exhibited his full genius.

Although Albert and Thomas based their work on a division between theology and philosophy, they did not tolerate contradictions between the two spheres. Faith and reason were two means for approaching the same truth. Since both were engendered by God and could not therefore be in disagreement, the Dominican scholars exerted great effort to reconcile any apparent conflicts. When all means had been exhausted, but the contradiction still remained, they conceded the fallability of reason and adopted the solution of faith. When, for example, the Scriptural doctrine of the voluntary and temporal creation of the world remained unreconciled with the Aristotelian notion of a necessary and eternal creation, the Dominicans, in contrast to the Averroists, abandoned Aristotle for the Bible. To Albert and Thomas one God guaranteed the unity of truth about which true faith and right reason could never disagree. Unlike the Averroists the Dominicans proposed a permanent synthesis of faith and reason.

Thomas Aquinas

Albert's and Thomas' monumental resolution of faith and reason cannot be viewed as exclusively the product of isolated geniuses, nor was it achieved without tremendous expenditure of intellectual labor. We have seen that they worked within the institutional framework of the university and profited from the efforts of their predecessors. The career of Thomas Aquinas in particular illustrates the academic milieu in which scholastic theology was nourished. Born in southern Italy to the family of the counts of Aquino, who were related to the Emperor Frederic II, Thomas received his elementary instruction at the monastery of Monte Cassino, the venerable birthplace of the Benedictine order. When his parents decided to further his education in the liberal arts at the university of Naples, recently founded by Frederic II, Thomas first came under the influence of the Dominican friars in these university surroundings and later decided to renounce his highborn heritage for the mendicant life, much to his family's chagrin and violent opposition. His Dominican colleagues must have quickly perceived signs of genius in their new convert because they soon sent him to study with their most illustrious scholar, Albert the Great. We are not certain whether Thomas first joined his master at Cologne or at Paris, but it was inevitable that a student of such talent would find his way to Paris. He entered the theological course at Saint-Jacques as a Biblical Bachelor, when he lectured probably on the books of Isaiah, Jeremiah, and Lamentations, and then passed on to the Bachelor of Sentences, when he produced his first mature work, the *Commentary to the Sentences of the Lombard.* Having completed the theological course and received a license to teach from the Chancellor of Notre-Dame by 1256, Thomas, along with his Franciscan contemporary Bonaventure, was ready for inception into the theological faculty. The moment, however, was hardly propitious because the friars and secular masters of theology were then deadlocked in a dispute over the right to strike. Finally Pope Alexander IV, who at that time favored the friars, specifically ordered the masters to admit Thomas and Bonaventure into their corporation, which act accorded full recognition to Thomas Aquinas as a professor of the university of Paris.

The mature years of Thomas' career until his death in 1274 were occupied with teaching theology either at Saint-Jacques in Paris or in numerous Dominican convents in Italy and finally at Naples. The written evidence of his teaching is immense (in one modern edition it comprises thirty-four volumes) and spans the whole spectrum of university activity. Many of his public lectures on authoritative texts were recorded in glosses and commentaries. Not only did Thomas continue to gloss the Scriptures and other theological treatises, but he produced a series of commentaries on Aristotle's major writings. These commentaries embody the scholastic activity of reading in an effort to assimilate the contents of the authorities, and in particular they indicate Thomas' great efforts to master the new philosophy of Aristotle. Moreover, as an active teacher, Thomas practiced about two disputations a week during the regular term (we possess the reports of over five hundred) and during the Christmas and Easter holidays numerous *disputationes de quolibet.* These debates afforded Thomas opportunity not only to solve pressing theological problems, but also to defend his position against the Averroists and the Franciscans. In the heat of these disputations Thomas forged the links of his theological system.

Thomas' most significant work was contained in the *summae.* Of the two he wrote, the *Summa contra Gentiles* was a rational defense of Christian theology and the *Summa theologica,* we remember, was the most complete and unified treatment of his thought. While these writings did not directly result from his academic activities, their essential elements were fashioned from teaching. Relying on the cooperation of his fellow theologians, he set down in his *Summa theologica* the fullest expression of his synthesis of theology and philosophy. His solutions to faith and reason were produced in the acrimonious disputes with the Franciscans on one hand and the Averroists on the other. Benefiting from the perspective of distant time, the poet Dante could view these controversies in softer light. In the glorious hierarchy of his *Paradiso* he found appropriate niches for Bonaventure the Franciscan (XII) and Siger of Brabant, the Averroist (X), but to Thomas Aquinas, the Dominican (X), the poet assigned the central seat of honor. Dante sensed the significance of Thomas' achievement. Since the appearance of the Gospel in the ancient world, Christians have pondered the relationship of their faith to the culture of Classical civilization. During the course of history numerous solutions to this problem have been proposed, but none was so bold as Thomas'. In his resolution of faith and reason he sought to unite revelation with Greek philosophy and Christianity with Classical culture in a durable synthesis. He sought to make Paris the heir of both Jerusalem and Athens. It must be remembered, however, that Thomas' solution did not dominate the later Middle Ages. In 1277 shortly after Thomas' death, the bishop of Paris under Franciscan influence condemned certain of his propositions with those of Siger of Brabant. In the following centuries the Dominican disciples of Thomas never gained clear ascendancy over rival systems of thought, but the true vitality of Thomas' system is indicated by its ability to outlast the Middle Ages. Although today Thomas is only one of many masters of Christian theology, he has enjoyed a greater vogue in modern times than ever in the Middle Ages.

Thomas' union between faith and reason may be better understood in the thirteenth century context of general security, peace and optimism. To this scene a flourishing economy of prosperous cities provided a sense of well-being. We have seen that one of the chief foundations for this stability was the mutual strength and cooperation of the French Capetians and the Papacy. When hostilities broke out between the French King Philip the Fair and Pope Boniface VIII, the times were out of joint. When the pope turned violently against the university of Paris, the former protégé of Rome, the masters were forced to side with their sovereign in his quarrel with the Papacy. Thus the university became the favorite daughter of the king of France, her former antagonist. The thirteenth century foundations of world order began to disintegrate in the following era, aggravated by pestilence, famine, and poverty. When in 1277 some of the elements of Thomas' synthesis were condemned by ecclesiastical authority, we have an event which parallels the political clash between King Philip and Pope Boniface. No longer did men have the courage to hold both faith and reason in their intellectual grasp, and their new systems revealed a great chasm between theology and philosophy. The thirteenth-century optimism dissolved into the despair of the late Middle Ages.

In one sense the medieval scholar lived in a world apart. Pursuing research, teaching students, and publishing conclusions in Latin to be read by colleagues, he never directly intended his more abstruse ideas and working procedures for the broader circles of society. In response to the tastes and pleasures of these classes, other writers produced a rich vernacular literature. For the bourgeoisie they recounted racy and cynically humorous tales of town life, known as the fabliaux. For entertaining the nobility they composed martial epics, lyrical love songs, and fanciful chivalric romances. Since literacy was the responsibility of the schools, it was hardly avoidable that some trace of the scholastic method would occasionally appear in these writings. When in the second half of the twelfth century, for example, a cleric named Andrew the Chaplain composed a manual on courtly love for a circle of noble ladies in Champagne, he arranged his arguments pro and con in a way suggestive of the school disputations. In the thirteenth century the most popular of all French chivalric romances was the *Romance of the Rose*, which treated aristocratic ideals in elaborate allegory. The second part of this poem, furnished by the Parisian bourgeois, Jean de Meung, amounts to a kind of *summa* and is permeated with scholastic terminology and techniques. Despite these occasional influences, the greater part of popular, vernacular literature of the Middle Ages remained untouched by the method of the schools. It must be remembered that throughout medieval times the term "laity" bore the connotation of one unlettered in Latin, the language of formal and advanced instruction. The principal channel by which the ideas and techniques of the schools reached a larger public was not vernacular literature, but the arts of architecture, sculpture, and glassmaking. Early in the twelfth century Honorius Augustodunensis voiced a commonplace when he designated art as the literature of the laity. Since the

GOTHIC ART

6

school was placed at the cathedral and the scholar was a cleric, particularly in France, the stone and glass of churches became the popular expression of scholastic culture.

The Birth of Gothic Architecture

One of the manifest signs of European economic expansion was the spectacular increase of stone church buildings which sprang up everywhere to serve as cathedrals, monasteries, and parish churches. Ralph Glaber, we have seen, noticed them in the eleventh century, but the phenomenon continued at an accelerated rate throughout the twelfth and thirteenth centuries. It strains our imagination today to grasp fully the resources and energy expended in this construction program. In France alone, according to one count, between 1180 and 1270 a population of less than eighteen million produced eighty churches of cathedral size and nearly five hundred abbeys. Or to focus on one local example in the thirteenth century, Chartres, a community of less than ten thousand souls, within one generation rebuilt its cathedral in truly monumental proportions. The competition to build and rebuild churches larger and higher than all others reached such a frenzy by the end of the thirteenth century that it may have seriously impaired the urban economy. Beauvais, for example, profited from its fertile region and its vigorous wool cloth industry to become the fastest growing and richest city in the royal domain, second only to Paris in the first half of the thirteenth century. By the end of the century, however, when other towns in northeast France enjoyed their greatest prosperity, Beauvais was in decline. Some have argued that the explanation lies in the decision of the bishop and chapter in 1247 to build the largest cathedral in Christendom, which consequently diverted funds that could have been better invested for the town's future. Just as the new cathedral placed an irreparable strain on Beauvais' economy, so the height of its vaults exceeded the strength of stone and began to crumble in 1284. Today it remains a truncated fragment of its intended grandeur and Beauvais, one of the minor cities of France. Admittedly, the success of Chartres and the failure of Beauvais were exceptional cases, but they nonetheless illustrate the high priority which medieval society gave to the building of churches.

Cathedral construction, such as at Chartres, was never completely confined to local enterprise. Dedicated to the Virgin Mary, this sanctuary claimed support from afar. Families from the Ile-de-France fixed their blazons on the windows to indicate their legacies to the church, and the whole south transept was decorated with sculpture and glass by the proud and troublesome house of Dreux, then counts of Brittany. Since Chartres was a royal bishopric, especially dependent upon the king as defender and benefactor, the

Capetians also patronized this church handsomely. Blanche of Castile, the queen mother and regent for her young son Louis IX, commissioned the windows of the north transept in unmistakable challenge to the rebellious Dreux's directly across the church. When the saintly Louis became of age, he himself lavished gifts upon churches with unprecedented enthusiasm. "Just as a scribe who has copied a manuscript and has illuminated it with gold and azure," affirmed his biographer with pride, "so the king illuminated his realm with beautiful abbeys and numerous Hôtel-Dieu's, convents of Preachers, Cordeliers and other religious orders." Important as was this aristocratic and royal support, it was not as crucial as that of the townsmen. Undoubtedly, a direct correspondence existed between the magnificence of edifices and the vitality of urban life. Sooner or later the bishop was compelled to rely on bourgeois cooperation for constructing the cathedral. At Chartres this dependence was mutual because the prosperity of the town's fair rested on the church's fame for attracting pilgrims. The merchant and trade guilds invested heavily in their cathedral and left their signatures on the windows. The wine merchants, for example, erected an exceptionally beautiful window which depicted their trade in three central medallions: the lower one showing a wine cart and its driver, the central portraying a man drawing wine from a cask, and the upper representing the most exalted use of wine in the eucharist. By elevating their vaults and increasing their towers, the men of one town competed with their neighbors, but they must also have been deeply impressed by the stark contrast between the permanence and splendor of their white stone church and the fragility and meanness of their dark wooden dwellings. From whatever direction one approached the town of Chartres, his first glimpse was of the spires and then of the cathedral mounting above the city rooftops (Plate III).

This burst of building energy in the twelfth century was accompanied by a new art style, subsequently named the Gothic by its enemies in the seventeenth century. Since the established style with which the Gothic competed was known as Romanesque, we should first consider the characteristics of Romanesque in order to understand the novelty of Gothic. With the return of comparative order and stability in the eleventh century, ecclesiastics desired to rebuild their churches with greater permanency. In the place of wooden roofs susceptible to fire, they erected stone vaults, which required massive masonry walls to support them. Since the thickness of these walls allowed little space for windows, light scarcely penetrated the interior. Romanesque churches, accompanied by strong bell towers, stood like fortresses of God against the Devil and his cohorts, an impression which suited the feudal aspects of their age. Since their chief builders were monks, the massive

III. The cathedral of Chartres seen from the southeast. (*Bildarchiv Foto Marburg 49,547*)

characteristics of the Romanesque style served monastic purposes well. The dense walls of the church spun a thick chrysalis about the altar which isolated and protected it from the world. In darkness the monks lit their liturgical tapers and filled the cavernlike vaults with the sacred music of their chants and prayers. On the inside the coarse stone surfaces were plastered over and painted with frescoes; without, the façades were decorated with exuberant and strongly expressive sculpture. Although Romanesque developed regional characteristics in areas such as northern Italy, southern France and Germany, as an artistic style it penetrated almost all of western Europe at one time or another. Romanesque was the universal art form which originated in the pre-urban era but retained its vitality well into the thirteenth century.

By contrast, the Gothic style was decidedly French by birth. It originated in the first half of the twelfth century in the Ile-de-France within a hundred-mile radius of Paris, a region heretofore undistinguished by artistic achievement. Within this vacuum the Gothic style germinated and emerged to challenge the supremacy of the Romanesque. Furthermore, its beginnings can be narrowed to the inspiration of one man in one church. Although the new style first appeared simultaneously in three different places, the best known was the royal abbey of Saint-Denis close to the north of Paris. Suger, Abbot of Saint-Denis, who was responsible for rebuilding the west façade and choir of this church between 1137 and 1144, exemplified the policy of cooperation between the church and the Capetian monarchy. Having proved himself an exceptionally able administrator of the abbey lands, Suger was chosen by the early Capetians to help manage the affairs of the kingdom. Faithfully and capably he served his monarchs by summoning ecclesiastical support for their projects, by rallying the nation in time of invasion, and by acting as regent when the king departed on a crusade. But the bonds between Saint-Denis and the royalty were even more intimate. Not only was the royal abbey the guardian of the French crown and insignia, but it was also the repository of the sacred relics of its namesake, the patron saint of France. Saint-Denis aspired to be the spiritual center of France; its banner, the oriflamme, was accepted as the standard of the kingdom. Suger promoted the claims of Saint-Denis by all available means of publicity. As integral parts of his program, he sponsored epic poetry which revived the memory of ancient Frankish kings and rebuilt the abbey in a new architectural style. When the new choir was dedicated in 1144, it was a national event attended by the royal family, the great barons and at least nineteen of the archbishops and bishops of the realm. In effect, the consecration of the abbey of Saint-Denis signified the baptism of the Gothic style.

For the next century and a half, the builders of northern France were busy developing the potentialities of the new style. Architectural historians generally divide Gothic art into two phases. The initial period, which ended with the twelfth century, is called Early Gothic and is represented by the beginnings of churches such as Saint-Denis, Sens, the west front of Chartres, Laon and Paris. At this stage the builders were occupied with finding solutions which were both technically feasible and aesthetically satisfying. Once these preliminary problems were resolved, the architects achieved a maturity and mastery in the thirteenth century in a stage called High Gothic and represented by churches such as the completed Chartres, Reims, and Amiens. Just as Suger, the chief lieutenant of the Capetians, initiated the new Gothic style, so the French royalty continued to claim responsibility for this artistic creation. For example, so close was Louis IX's supervision of the churches built in the Ile-de-France during his reign that historians designate this phase of Gothic architecture, best seen in the Sainte-Chapelle at Paris, as the Court style. Born in the cradle of the Capetian domain, the Gothic style spread throughout Europe with the political fortunes of France. This "French style" (*opus francigenum*), as it frequently was known, appeared in southern France with the Albigensian crusade from the north (for example, at Saint-Nazaire in Carcassonne) and in southern Italy (for example, Lucera cathedral) with the French penetration into the Mediterranean. The mendicant orders, which were always in close contact with the university of Paris, also adopted the new style for their new churches throughout Christendom. We have seen that the Franciscans at Bologna were one of the first in Italy to boast of a new "French" church. Because of the *éclat* of French culture in the thirteenth century, the Gothic style soon came into vogue throughout western Europe.

As is often true of artistic creation, the constituent elements were not new, but the Gothic revolution consisted of their combined use and total effect. Such devices as the ribbed vault and pointed arch, once considered the dominant characteristics of Gothic, can now be traced to Muslim, Burgundian and Norman antecedents. Art historians today tend to emphasize the windows as the essential feature of Gothic architecture. In contrast to the Romanesque builder who preferred the cover of darkness, the Gothic architect directed all of his technical skill to flooding his church with light. Following its source, he raised the ceilings higher and higher to produce an overpowering sense of verticality. In an effort to capture every ray of the sun, he shaved his walls as thin as possible and opened all available space to glass. Where the structural requirements demanded wall support, even here he faced the wall with columns and arches to produce the impression of layers of lace. Unlike the massive, confining, and isolating effect of Romanesque walls, the Gothic shell is delicate, diaphanous, and luminous, enveloping the church in an intangible mantle. Indeed, the Gothic wall is scarcely apparent—all is resplendent light.

To provide for these windows the Gothic builder was obliged to solve a number of difficult technical problems. We must remember that his elementary unit of construction was the simple stone block, yet like his Romanesque predecessor he wished to create a permanent edifice composed of stone ceilings as well as walls. Stone vaults hundreds of feet above the floor were structurally antithetical to thin walls open to glass. One major solution was the ribbed vault, which carried the downward thrust of the ceiling on a framework of ribs. Since the vaulting between these ribs could be reduced to light stone, the whole weight was concentrated on a small number of piers. Because the edifice's weight was chiefly borne by this structural skeleton, the wide spaces in the walls could be opened to windows. Along with these ribs the Gothic architect also utilized the pointed arch, which solved technical problems where the sides of vaults were not unilateral, and which likewise contributed to the height of his building. The thrust of a stone vault, however, is not only downwards, but also outward. To carry this load the builder devised the system of flying buttresses, which distributed the weight gracefully from vault to rib, to strut, to pier buttress, and then to the ground. By means of the ribbed skeleton and the flying buttresses, most of the roof's weight was transferred to the outside of the church, leaving the interior unencumbered and free for windows. Thus the Gothic interior affords the sensation of weightlessness as well as verticality, and again, the primary justification for the peculiarities of the flying buttress was the full enjoyment of windows. As the builders solved their problems, their boldness increased. The Early Gothic vaults of Paris and Laon did not exceed eighty feet in height; the High Gothic churches jumped to 120 feet at Chartres and 140 feet at Amiens. When the vaults at Beauvais neared 160 feet, in what was intended to be the largest church of western Christendom, as we have seen, the tensile limit of stone was exceeded, and the ceiling crashed down. Without new materials such as structural steel or reinforced concrete, the Gothic architect could go no farther.

If the Gothic artist esteemed his cathedral for its windows, we shall find it difficult to appreciate his visual experience because most medieval windows of French churches have since disappeared through the ravages of neglect, distaste and revolution. Although isolated examples have survived, the total effect of the light produced by the windows has been lost. The one major exception which saves us from complete blindness to what the medieval man saw is the cathedral of Chartres. Of the 186 original windows 152 have survived, and there we can still experience the sensation of

Gothic light. In the west façade dating from the twelfth century are found early examples of the glassmakers, reminiscent of the first windows which Suger placed in Saint-Denis. These windows are distinguished by brilliant color and intricate craftsmanship, as if the artists were working with precious jewels. As the glassmakers gained confidence in the thirteenth century, they enlarged the proportions to create bold, dramatic figures for the clerestory windows in the uppermost part of the church. Their skill reached a climax in the three spectacular rose windows of the west, north and south fronts whose lavish colors rival natural flowers. The windows of Chartres are most remarkable for the quality of their color. Like small children the medieval glassmakers were unafraid of pigment and used it with enthusiasm. Successful with the purity of their blues and the vividness of their reds, they flooded the church's interior with a violet hue which fluctuates with the temperament of the sky outside. Each piece of glass is not merely a surface of reflected color but rather a source of radiant light, which explains why the effect of medieval stained glass cannot be reproduced by photograph or painting but only by glass itself. Until the last ray of light has faded from the sky the windows of Chartres retain their incandescence.

The Schools and Gothic Art

Fostered by the same political stability and economic prosperity, the schools and universities and Gothic art were products of the same culture. Particularly in France the list of the flourishing schools coincided remarkably with that of Gothic monuments, because both sprang from the vitality of urban life. The correlation in time is equally significant. Abelard and Suger, the one an innovator in theology, the other in art, knew each other well. At Chartres the two towers of the west front (the northernmost was redone in the sixteenth century) and the sculpture between were created during the mid-years of the twelfth century not long after the school of Bernard had flourished. Notre-Dame on the Ile-de-la-Cité of Paris was also advantageously situated to witness the growth of the universities. (Plate II) The first stone layed in 1163 and the last flying buttress completed after 1300, the life of Notre-Dame spanned the crucial decades of the university. The imposing west façade was begun about 1200; by 1250 the towers were finished, a few years before Bonaventure and Thomas Aquinas were incepted into the faculty of theology. Chronologically, the towers of Notre-Dame and the scholastic theologians were graduates of the same class. We remember that when the Parisian theologian Peter the Chanter wished to depict the scholastic techniques of reading, disputing and preaching, he resorted to an architectural analogy. Reciprocally, when the Gothic artist conceived of his monuments, he thought of them in scholastic terms.

In an elementary fashion the Gothic architect was indebted to the school. His was necessarily a learned craft which involved difficult technical problems. Within the academic framework, architectural skill was considered a part of geometry whose principles resolved many problems involving lines of force and rays of light. Above all, the architect's supreme norm was the rule of proportionality, which was closely related to the conception of music, also one of the liberal arts. In the Middle Ages men became fascinated with numerical relationships which produced harmony in music and proportion in geometry. The guiding spirit of these disciplines is well illustrated in one of the few sketch books of a Gothic architect which have survived. Villard of Honnecourt, who worked in the first half of the thirteenth century, indicated his tastes and preferences in drawings of the churches of Laon, Chartres and Reims. The harmonies of Laon's towers, for example, elicited his particular praise. By sketching a decorative statue of a lion, he illustrated how natural appearance was subject to geometric rules. Even in sculpture, proportion was the dominant principle of the Gothic style. The crowd of sculpture, therefore, which decorated the Gothic exteriors gives the impression of serenity and balance, an almost monumental quality dictated by the architectural vision. As the medieval architect solved his technical problems, he saw his craft in larger perspective. The twelfth-century scholars who specialized in the quadrivium and cosmology conceived of God as the great architect of the universe holding the geometer's compass, and in the words of Scripture ordering "all things in measure and number and weight" (Wisdom 11:20). Just as the great Geometer created the world in order and harmony, so the Gothic architect, in his small way, attempted to fashion God's earthly abode according to the supreme principles of proportion and beauty.

Not only did the architect receive instruction from the liberal arts masters, but he also derived inspiration and meaning from the theologians. Since his ultimate concern was the windows and the light they introduced, he could not avoid the theological significance of light. Under the influence of Plato, the Church Father Augustine, we remember, considered the problem of knowledge in metaphorical terms of illumination. Divine illumination is to our minds what the sun is to our eyes. This simile fashioned by Augustine was repeated by his Franciscan followers in the thirteenth century. While, technically speaking, the theologians regarded divine illumination as immaterial and distinct from physical light, the architects could not overlook the implications of this metaphor for their endeavors. Moreover, inspired by a common Platonism, the doctrine of divine illumination was taught by another ancient authority, the converted Greek philosopher Dionysius, who medieval Frenchmen claimed was none other than their own Saint Denis. His works were widely read and commented on by theologians such as Hugh of Saint-Victor and Thomas Aquinas. No wonder then that in constructing a church in honor of this philosopher of light, close attention was paid to the windows placed in the choir and the nave. Suger revelled in the glory of his sacred glass which miraculously brightened the choir of his church. Lest the worshipper should miss the full import, he inscribed a verse on the doors, which proclaimed that this light lifted the mind from the material world and directed it toward the true light coming from Christ the door. Because of a common light metaphysics inspired by Augustine and Dionysius, Hugh of Saint-Victor and Thomas Aquinas listed among their standards of beauty not only proportion but also luminosity.

Beauty, however, is also a matter of taste, and from the Renaissance until the nineteenth century Gothic art was unfashionable (hence the term Gothic, meaning barbaric). Whether Gothic is beautiful or not, most art critics agree that it usually possessed meaning. While the bizarre figures on Romanesque churches may have been the result of the sculptor's caprice, the Gothic architect, sculptor or glassmaker was not content merely to delight the senses, but was always careful to convey meaning and instruction. From its foundations Gothic art was a form of teaching. In the architectural realm, however, modern art historians have not been able to agree fully on the lessons imparted by the builders. Some interpret the churches as the palaces of Mary, others as expressions of Christ's body, and many envisage Gothic churches fashioned by medieval townsmen as the city of Heaven. For this reason the entrance of the west façade is seen to resemble the gate to a Roman town. Whatever the differences of opinion over architecture, more agreement has been achieved in sculpture and stained glass. Consensus here has enabled the development of medieval iconography, which studies the meaning of artistic images.

The exterior of a Gothic church was decorated with an amazing profusion of statuary, especially around the portals of the west, north, and south façades where the artist placed row after row of saints and confessors, prophets and apostles, kings and bishops, monks and virgins, peasants and beasts, and still more. Within the church the stained-glass windows multiplied these hosts of figures. Chartres, for example, is adorned with over 1,800 pieces of sculpture and with many more glass images, and these numbers are even exceeded at other High Gothic churches. Yet closer inspection will change this bewildering forest of figures into a storyland of familiar themes. The medieval artists and their theological advisors combed the pages of the Old and New Testaments and the literature of saints' lives for personages and stories to depict in stone and glass.

These Biblical histories and saints' biographies, in addition to themes drawn from theology, morality, daily living, and natural history, form distinct "cycles" or groups which follow their own traditions. A modern art historian therefore finds it possible to isolate one of these cycles, to study its representations on various churches, and to discern underlying meaning, which has resulted in the rediscovery of a common iconographical language through the world of church art. Certain devices and signs denoted special meaning. For example, a cross superimposed on a halo signified either Christ or God the Father. Bare feet indicated either an apostle or one of the Godhead. The Apostle Peter was usually depicted with bushy hair, a short beard, and holding some keys, while the apostle Paul was bald with a long beard and generally carried a sword. The illiterate man could read these signs like characters of writing and understand the sculpture and glass of the cathedrals. Iconography was the language in which the artists taught people throughout Christendom.

To impart right faith and good conduct were the chief purposes for which medieval artists created their images. Two different kinds of examples may be taken to illustrate these endeavors. Among the schemes to teach morality, the Gothic artists often allegorized the virtues and their opposing vices in bas-relief figures such as we find on the west fronts of Paris, Amiens, and Chartres. The victorious virtues pose serenely with their respective symbols emblazoned on their shields, while underneath the more interesting vices act out their characteristic misdeeds. At Paris, for example, courage is seated above in armor with a lion etched on her shield while below cowardliness is represented by a knight who has discarded his sword in flight from a hare. The vices in particular were drawn from everyday life which would be immediately recognized by the passerby. Thus Lust admires herself in a mirror, Avarice weighs out her gold, Despair runs herself through with a sword, and Discord is depicted by a brawl between a husband and a wife. Of all iconographical cycles of Gothic art the best-developed theme was the Last Judgment (Plate IV). With dramatic effectiveness the sculptors represented that last day when the angels will sound the trumpet and the dead will rise from their tombs to be apportioned their just deserts in Heaven or in Hell. Above all Christ was depicted as the supreme Judge seated in awesome majesty. This moving scene, which may be found on almost every Gothic cathedral, likewise served a moral purpose. The saintly Hugh, bishop of Lincoln, for example, used the Last Judgment sculpture at Fontevrault as an opportunity to warn the future King John of England of the just punishment which awaited wicked monarchs, but we know that the king unfortunately did not profit from this sermon. These judgment scenes, such as the one on the south portal of the Strasbourg cathedral, also served as the backdrop for courts of canon law to remind

IV. The central portal of the western façade of Notre-Dame of Paris (*Bildarchiv Foto Marburg 183,452*)

earthly judges and contestants that their immediate decisions would some day be reviewed by the supreme Judge.

In addition to the exalted themes of religion and morality, the occupations and skills of ordinary life were also represented in Gothic art. For example, peasant labors in the fields may be found on many important churches. At Amiens, where the cycle was most beautifully executed, the farmer may be seen threshing grain, dressing vines, pressing grapes, warming his feet by the fire, and engaging in many other activities. His entire seasonal calendar was depicted according to the signs of the zodiac. But human occupations included not only the toil of the hands, but also the efforts of the mind. Since the cathedral was often the seat of a school, we should expect to find images of the seven liberal arts on the cathedrals of the leading centers of learning such as Paris, Chartres, and Laon. Reflecting the preeminence of Chartres in the early twelfth century, the artists there created the first and best developed cycle of the liberal arts. At the same time that the Chancellor Thierry composed the *Heptateuchon*, his manual on the seven liberal arts, which he bequeathed to the chapter of Chartres, the sculptors depicted them as female figures, each seated above her chief authority (Plate V). To follow them in order around the portal from left to right: Dialectic holds a stinging scorpion; Rhetoric makes an oratorical geste; Geometry traces with a compass on a tablet across her knees; Arithmetic counts with her fingers; Astronomy gazes upwards; and Music, most easily identified, plays on her bells. At the bottom right, Grammar, whom John of Salisbury described as "the first nurse of the whole study of letters" is fashioned as a venerable woman holding a book in one hand and the proverbial switch in the other (Plate VI). Obviously pedagogical discipline has been a perennial problem because one of the boys at her feet is pulling the other's hair. The authorities are represented as scribes at work at their desks. Although they cannot be visually distinguished, we may identify Donatus below Grammar, Cicero below Rhetoric, Aristotle (who is dipping his pen) below Dialectics, and the others from Thierry's manual. "Puny dwarfs perched on the shoulders of giants," we remember, was Bernard of Chartres' phrase for illustrating the importance of ancient authority in medieval learning. Not only were the twelfth-century sculptors of Chartres careful to accompany each liberal art with her authority, but the thirteenth century glassmakers still remembered Bernard's image. In the south transept patronized by the family of Dreux, we may find four towering figures of the major Old Testament prophets, each with a smaller Gospel writer seated upon his shoulders. Like all wisdom, the New Testament Gospels benefited from the stature of Old Testament authority.

The artists at Laon and Paris also added an eighth figure to

V. The southern portal of the western façade of the cathedral of Chartres
(*Bildarchiv Foto Marburg 30061*)

the liberal arts, philosophy, who was represented as a woman according to the description found in Boethius, a writer of the sixth century. She was characteristically depicted with her head in the clouds and with a ladder against her chest which indicated the steps of philosophic knowledge. At Chartres, the liberal arts were arranged around the central figure of the infant Christ seated on the lap of His mother, while at Notre-Dame in Paris, along with philosophy, they were carved into the pedestal of a statue of Christ where they may be seen today in restoration. These positions illustrate the theologian's teaching that the liberal arts were not independent disciplines, but served divine knowledge represented by Christ. Modern scholars have attributed different meanings to this statue of Christ, which occupies the centralmost position on the west front of Paris (Plate IV). Similar figures may be found at Chartres and Reims, but the most beautiful example is the famous *Beau Dieu* at

VI. Representations of music and grammar with the authorities, Pythagorus and Donatus, on the southern portal of the western façade of the cathedral of Chartres (*Bildarchiv Foto Marburg 35410*)

Amiens (Plate VII). Because he carries a book and because he stands above the arts at Paris, some scholars interpret him as Christ the Teacher. If this view is correct, we have an expression of Bonaventure's conception of Christ as the Teacher of all. Here Christ stands as the exemplary Master of the university of Paris.

The cycles of liberal arts, philosophy and Christ the Teacher suggest close relations between the schoolmen and the Gothic artists, but this scholastic influence may be traced not only in specific themes but also indirectly in artistic method and procedure. We have seen that the medieval masters and students tended to form schools of thought in which it often becomes difficult to distinguish the teacher from his circle. Similarly, Gothic sculptors organized workshops in which they supervised and perfected the craft of their assistants. From the twelfth-century sculpture of Chartres, for example, we can distinguish one chief and four subordinate artists, each with their own assistants, and at Reims in the thirteenth century one anonymous sculptor of genius left his mark on the work of many others. Even in architecture the existence of schools is probable because we can discern striking relationships, for example, between the porches of the cathedrals at Laon and the Chartres transepts. Villard of Honnecourt's sketchbook itself was a product of the Gothic workshop. Originally Villard made some drawings for a trip to Hungary, but later converted his notebook into a textbook for his students. It remained in the *atelier* after his death where notes and drawings were added by at least two anonymous masters. Never intended for publication, its fortuitous survival gives us a rare glimpse into the workaday world of a medieval artist. In the twelfth century most of the Gothic architects and artists remain hidden in anonymity, but as they perfected their techniques during the thirteenth century they reveal themselves more readily, so that we know the names of the several architects who worked on Reims and Amiens. One fashionable member of this class was Peter of Montreuil, whose chief work was the south portal of Notre-Dame and who had inscribed on his tomb at Saint-Germain-des-Prés the academic title, Doctor of Masons.

Not only did these Gothic architects and artists work within their own schools, but they also profited from the experience of their competitors. In their buildings, sculpture or glass, they kept an eye on achievements of their fellow workers. Like the masters in the schools, they sometimes rejected, sometimes incorporated the solutions of others into their work. Thus a particular architectural device, such as the rose window, was created according to the rhythm of yeses and noes of the *Sic et Non* of Abelard or a thirteenth-century disputation. We can trace these experiments, rejections and modifications in the development of the rose window at Saint-Denis, Notre-Dame of Paris, Laon, Chartres, Amiens, with a final resolution

VII. The *Beau Dieu* of the cathedral of Amiens (*Bildarchiv Foto Marburg 32142*)

at Reims. As in the liberal arts, law and theology, the final achievements of Gothic art were essentially social creations.

The schoolmen solved their problems and recorded the results in their *summae*. In the same way the Gothic architects and artists perfected and incorporated their techniques in their churches. With excellent reason, therefore, the Gothic cathedral has often been called an artistic *summa*. Just as the juristic and theological *summae* attempted to encompass the whole body of relevant knowledge, so the medieval artist tried to create in sculpture and windows images of knowledge necessary to the Christian. All of the ramifications of right faith and good conduct were made visible to the medieval beholder through the numerous iconographical cycles, which did not express the pure erudition of the professional theologian, but rather the interpretation of essential knowledge for the people. Since the cathedrals were the *summae* to be read by the ordinary man, we should be prepared for the blending of childlike candor and *naiveté* with artistic proficiency and sophistication. The artists did not always teach profound theological speculation, but more often the stories of the Bible and the saints, and so helped the theologian reach the people. Despite this popular character of Gothic art, the impress of the theological professor is still evident. Just as the masters' *summae* organized all knowledge into a logical and systematic whole, so the cathedrals focused all details on a unifying theme. Here the role of the Gothic architect dominated all others. The sculpture, as we have seen, was envisaged in geometric and architectural terms. Among the successive rows of angels and martyrs, within the clusters of confessors and apostles, each single figure was fashioned with regard to the total conception. All was controlled by the comprehensive and coherent thought of the architect. Like the *Golden Summa* of Hostiensis and the *Summa theologica* of Thomas Aquinas the Gothic cathedral had a place for everything and everything found its place (Plate IV). Again, it was Thomas Aquinas who most explicitly noted the close correspondence between the architect and the professor. Following Aristotle, Thomas envisaged the architect as the workmaster who supervises the individual craftsmen and artists working on the building. Just as the architect orders these artisan skills according to his over-all scheme, so the philosopher recognizes the goals of subsidiary disciplines and organizes all knowledge in its logical place.

In art we often catch a brief but revealing glimpse of the unconscious temperament of an age. In a sense, art captures our image when we are unaware. Just as Greek sculpture reflects the traits and development of ancient culture, so the stone and glass of Gothic art offers an oblique but penetrating image of the thirteenth century. There is something about the grandeur of the figures of Christ in Judgment (Plate IV) and the serenity of the *Beau Dieu*

VIII. The smiling angel of the cathedral of Reims (*Bildarchiv Foto Marburg 184,178*)

(Plate VII) that reveals an age confident in its powers and secure in its stability. In the culminating sculpture of Reims this confidence breaks into a smile—the half-smile of quiet contentment (Plate VIII). The thirteenth century was one of those rare ages of the smile justified by human achievement. It contrasts dramatically with the distorted visage of the succeeding centuries when Christ was depicted in stark realism upon His cross bearing the agony and disasters of His people. This passage from the triumphant Christ to the suffering Jesus is only one of the many signs of the subsequent gloom and despair of the late Middle Ages.

SUGGESTIONS FOR FURTHER READING

The most comprehensive and recent bibliography for the subject of this book may be found in Frederick B. Artz, *The Mind of the Middle Ages*, 3rd ed. rev. (New York: Alfred A. Knopf, 1965). Richard Kay, *The Middle Ages in Paperback* (Lawrence, Kansas: Coronado Press, 1969)* is also a useful bibliography of works available in paperback.

Achille Luchaire, *Social France at the Time of Philip Augustus* (New York: Harper Torchbooks, 1967)* presents an older but reliable account of the French social background in the twelfth and thirteenth centuries.

The basic study of medieval education in any language is Hastings Rashdall, edited by F. M. Powicke and A. B. Emden, *The Universities of Europe in the Middle Ages* (Oxford: Oxford University Press, 1936), 3 volumes. Profiting from this work, Charles Homer Haskins has published some stimulating lectures, *The Rise of Universities* (Ithaca: Cornell Great Seal Books, 1957).* Lowrie J. Daly, *The Medieval University, 1200–1400* (New York: Sheed & Ward, 1961) is a popular account, and Pearl Kibre has contributed two specialized studies, *The Nations in Medieval Universities* (Cambridge, Mass.: Mediaeval Academy of America, 1948) and *Scholarly Privileges in the Middle Ages* (Cambridge, Mass.: Mediaeval Academy of America, 1962). Gordon Leff, *Paris and Oxford Universities in the Thirteenth and Fourteenth Centuries* (New York: John Wiley & Sons, 1968)* summarizes recent scholarship. Lynn Thorndike, *University Records and Life in the Middle Ages* (New York: Columbia University Press, 1949) and Helene Wieruszowski, *The Medieval University* (Princeton: Van Nostrand Anvil Original, 1966)* are collections of sources in translation. An exciting introduction to the student poetry of the Goliards may be found in Helen Waddell, *The Wandering Scholars* (Garden City, N.Y.: Doubleday Anchor Books, 1955).* Jacques Le Goff, *Les intellectuels au moyen âge* (Paris: Editions du Seuil, 1960)* has interesting interpretations, which I have adopted in this essay, and is exquisitely illustrated.

Martin Grabmann, *Die Geschichte der scholastischen Methode* (Freiburg im Breisgau: Herder, 1909; Berlin: Akademie-Verlag, 1957), 2 volumes, is the classic study of the theme of this book. R. R. Bolgar, *The Classical Heritage and its Beneficiaries: From the Carolingian Age to the End of the Renaissance* (New York: Harper Torchbooks, 1964)* is a helpful introduction to the liberal arts in the Middle Ages. There are as yet few works on the study of medieval law for the general reader. Hermann Kantorowicz,

*Denotes books obtainable in inexpensive paperbound editions.

Studies in the Glossators of the Roman Law (Cambridge: Cambridge University Press, 1938) is a technical investigation, but Stephan Kuttner has discussed the general approach of the canonists in a lecture published as *Harmony from Dissonance: An Interpretation of Medieval Canon Law* (Latrobe, Pennsylvania: Archabbey Press, 1961). G. LeBras, Ch. Lefebvre, and J. Rambaud, *L'âge classique, 1140–1378: Sources et théorie du droit* (Paris: Sirey, 1965) is the most up-to-date survey of canon law.

A good number of books have been written on the general history of thought in the Middle Ages. One of the first, Henry Osborn Taylor, *The Medieval Mind,* 4th ed. (Cambridge, Mass.: Harvard University Press, 1949), 2 volumes, remains a classic because of the author's intimate knowledge of and feeling for the writings he treats. Most of these general histories are written from the viewpoint of philosophy. Josef Pieper, *Scholasticism* (New York: McGraw-Hill Book Co., 1964),* David Knowles, *The Evolution of Medieval Thought* (New York: Vintage Books, 1962),* Gordon Leff, *Medieval Thought: St. Augustine to Ockham* (Baltimore: Penguin Books, 1958),* Paul Vignaux, *Philosophy in the Middle Ages: An Introduction* (New York: Meridian Books, 1959),* and F. Copleston, *Medieval Philosophy* (Garden City, N.Y.: Doubleday Anchor Books, 1963),* 2 volumes, are recent surveys. Aimé Forest, F. van Steenberghen, and M. de Gandillac, *Le mouvement doctrinale du XIᵉ au XIVᵉ siècle* (Paris: Bloud and Gay, 1956) is comprehensive and has detailed bibliographies. Almost everything written by Étienne Gilson on the subject is worth the student's attention. His *The Spirit of Mediaeval Philosophy* (New York: Charles Scribner's Sons, 1936),* *History of Christian Philosophy in the Middle Ages* (New York: Random House, 1955), and *Reason and Revelation in the Middle Ages* (New York: Charles Scribner's Sons, 1938)* are of general interest. Jean Leclercq, *The Love of Learning and the Desire for God* (New York: Mentor, 1962)* is the classic introduction to monastic learning.

Because of its vitality and originality, the twelfth century has attracted the interest of many scholars. Charles Homer Haskins in his pioneer study *The Renaissance of the Twelfth Century* (New York: Meridian Books, 1957)* initiated the discussion. R. W. Southern, *The Making of the Middle Ages* (New Haven: Yale University Press, 1961)* has offered a stimulating interpretation of the total picture of society and thought in the eleventh and twelfth centuries. Philippe Wolff, *The Cultural Awakening* (New York: Pantheon Books, 1968) and Christopher Brooke, *The Twelfth Century Renaissance* (New York: Harcourt, Brace and World, 1970) are recent and biographical approaches to the period. G. Paré, A. Brunet, and P. Tremblay, *La renaissance du XIIᵉ siècle; Les écoles et l'enseignement* (Paris, Ottawa: Vrin, 1933) and M.-D. Chenu, *Nature, Man and Society in the Twelfth Century. Essays on New Theological Perspectives in the Latin West* (Chicago: University of Chicago Press, 1968) offer penetrating insights. Beryl Smalley, *The Study of the Bible in the Middle Ages* (Notre Dame, Ind.: University of Notre Dame Press, 1964)* focuses primarily on the twelfth century. R. W. Southern, *Saint Anselm and his Biographer* (Cambridge: Cambridge University Press, 1966), J. G. Sikes, *Abailard* (Cambridge: Cambridge University Press, 1932; New York: Russell and Russell Publishers, 1965), Étienne Gilson, *Heloise and Abelard* (Ann Arbor: University of Michigan Paperbacks, 1960),* and John W. Baldwin, *Masters, Princes,* and *Merchants: The Social Views of Peter the Chanter and his Circle* (Princeton: Princeton University Press, 1970), 2 volumes, are studies of important figures in the twelfth century.

There are fewer studies that encompass the thirteenth century as a whole. Ferdinand van Steenberghen's controversial *Siger de Brabant* (Louvain: Editions de l'Institut Supérieur de Philosophie, 1931) comes closest to this scope. His conclusions are summarized in English in his *Aristotle in the West* (Louvain: E. Nauwelaerts, 1955). Most scholars have tended to focus on dominant figures. Étienne Gilson, *The Philosophy of Saint Bonaventure* (Paterson, N. J.: St. Anthony Guild Press, 1965) is the classic but controversial study, and J. Guy Bougerol, *Introduction to the Works of Bonaventure* (Paterson, N. J.: St. Anthony Guild Press, 1964) is the most recent study of this scholastic. From the vast ocean of scholarly literature on Thomas Aquinas, we may select only a few works. Angelus Walz, Paul Novarina, *Saint Thomas d'Aquin* (Louvain, Paris: Béatrice-Nauwelaerts, 1962) is the best biography. M.-D. Chenu, *Toward Understanding Saint Thomas* (Chicago: Henry Regnery Co., 1964) places Thomas in his university context. F. C. Copleston, *Aquinas* (Baltimore: Penguin, 1955),* and J. Maritain, *Saint Thomas Aquinas* (New York: Meridian Books, 1958),* are readily available interpretations of his thought.

For an illustration of how the medieval lawyers and theologians disputed and produced a doctrine of practical significance, see John W. Baldwin, *The Medieval Theories of the Just Price: Romanists, Canonists, and Theologians in the Twelfth and Thirteenth Centuries, Transactions of the American Philosophical Society,* vol. 49 (Philadelphia, 1959).

The original sources for medieval intellectual history were, of course, written in Latin, for which we have a good number of modern editions in the original language. Only a bare fraction, and not always the most important, have been translated into English. For the twelfth century, translations exist for Anselm of Canterbury, *Proslogium; Monologium; and Cur Deus Homo* (LaSalle, Ill.: Open Court Publishing Co., 1954),* *Truth, Freedom, and Evil: Three Philosophic Dialogues* (New York: Harper Torchbooks, 1967),* *The Story of Abelard's Adversities* (Toronto: Pontifical Institute of Mediaeval Studies, 1964),* Bernard of Clairvaux, *Letters* (Chicago: Henry Regnery Co., 1953), Hugh of Saint-Victor, *Didascalicon* (New York: Columbia University Press, 1961), *On the Sacraments of the Christian Faith* (Cambridge, Mass.: Mediaeval Academy of America, 1951), and John of Salisbury, *Metalogicon* (Berkeley: University of California Press, 1962).* In the thirteenth century, some of Bonaventure's shorter treatises have been translated: *Breviloquium* (St. Louis: B. Herder Book Co., 1947), *De reductione artium ad theologiam* (St. Bonaventure, New York: St. Bonaventure University Press, 1940), and *Mind's Road to God* (New York: Library of Liberal Arts, 1953).* *The Basic Writings of Saint Thomas Aquinas* (New York: Random House, 1945), 2 volumes, is a useful selection of the vast body of Thomas' works.

Henry Adams in his *Mont-Saint-Michel and Chartres* (Garden City, N.Y.: Doubleday Anchor Books, 1959; New York: Mentor Books, Collier Books; Boston: Houghton Mifflin Co.)* was one of the first to try to see literature, art, and history as a whole, a task which he accomplished in an impressionistic and stimulating way. Otto Von Simson, *The Gothic*

Cathedral (New York: Harper Torchbooks)* attempts to interpret the intellectual content of Gothic art, and Erwin Panofsky, *Gothic Architecture and Scholasticism* (New York: Meridian Books, 1957)* relates the mental habits of the architects with the manner of scholastic thinking. For a balanced and brief account of the cathedrals of Chartres, Reims, and Amiens, see Hans Jantzen, *High Gothic* (New York: Pantheon Books, 1962). Emile Male, *The Gothic Image* (New York: Harper Torchbooks, 1958)* remains the classic study of iconography in the thirteenth century. Adolf Katzenellenbogen's *The Sculptural Programs of Chartres Cathedral* (New York: W.W. Norton & Co., 1964)* and *Allegories of the Virtues and Vices in Mediaeval Art* (New York: W.W. Norton & Co., 1964)* are penetrating studies of these important subjects. Allen Temko, *Notre-Dame of Paris* (New York: The Viking Press)* is an account somewhat in the Adams manner. Robert Branner, *St. Louis and the Court Style in Gothic Architecture* (London: A. Zwemmer, 1965) traces royal influence on the development and dissemination of Gothic art.

INDEX